Negotiating in the Age of Integrity

Other Titles in the Series

MAKE THE RIGHT DECISION EVERY TIME
by Roger Dawson

SELLING WITH NLP
by Kerry Johnson

THE NEW DYNAMICS OF WINNING:
GAIN THE MIND-SET OF A CHAMPION
by Denis Waitley

EMPIRES OF THE MIND:
LESSONS TO LEAD AND SUCCEED IN A KNOWLEDGE-
BASED WORLD
by Denis Waitley

NLP: THE NEW TECHNOLOGY OF ACHIEVEMENT
edited by Steve Andreas and Charles Faulkner
The NLP Comprehensive Training Team

TRANSITIONS: MAKING SENSE OF LIFE'S CHANGES
by William Bridges

Negotiating in the Age of Integrity

A complete guide to negotiating win/win in business and life

Wayne Berry

NICHOLAS BREALEY
PUBLISHING

LONDON

First published in Great Britain by
Nicholas Brealey Publishing Limited in 1996
21 Bloomsbury Way
London WC1A 2TH

© Wayne Berry 1995, 1996

ISBN 1-85788-123-0 .

British Library Cataloguing in Publication Data
A catalogue record for this book is available from the
British Library.

Printed in Great Britain by Redwood Books Ltd, Trowbridge

Contents

Contents (Cont'd)

Preface

Let me give you a little of my background so you know where I'm coming from.

Firstly, I have a confession to make. Most of the ideas I'll be sharing with you in this book are not mine! I was not born a highly skilled and highly successful negotiator. Almost everything I now know about negotiating and getting along with other people, I've learnt from other people whom I've been fortunate enough to know during my life so far.

For example, in the early 1980s I was privileged to meet an intriguing Jewish negotiator from New York. He was an adviser to American Presidents, had negotiated some real life and death situations with terrorists and had written a book called *You Can Negotiate Anything!* Perhaps you've read it too?

I'd read his book a few years earlier and then got to spend about a week with him as I promoted him in Australia. His name was Herb Cohen. He smoked foul smelling cigars all day and had a wry sense of humour that I'd never encountered before. I came to respect him enormously. To him negotiating was just a game. A game to enjoy and he was one of the funniest speakers I'd ever heard. I remember thinking at the time, "Wow, if I only knew a fraction of what this man knows, I really could negotiate anything."

The subject of negotiating had always fascinated me and I longed to be good at it. And then in the mid 1980s, I was privileged to meet and work with another great negotiating skills trainer and speaker, the author of another bestselling book called *You Can Get Anything You Want, But You'll Have to Do More Than Ask — The Secrets of Power Negotiating*. His name was Roger Dawson.

I brought Roger to Australia, New Zealand and South East Asia many times during the mid to late 1980s to conduct his seminars and he became a firm friend. Roger is one of the most generous people I have ever met. On a recent visit to LA, Roger picked me up at the airport in his Rolls Royce and then gave me the keys to his Corvette Stingray and his home to use during my stay!

So, after more than 25 years in business — both buying and selling — I've been personally involved in negotiating many millions of dollars worth of contracts. I have studied negotiating skills, styles and techniques intensively for more than 15 of those years, so in this book I speak from real life personal experience.

So do I know it all? Certainly I do not! I'm a student of life and I continue to learn every day. In particular, in recent years since I have started to study the relatively new technology of change and human communication, called Neuro Linguistic Programming or NLP, my learning and distinctions have accelerated even more. I have also been teaching negotiating skills workshops almost every month now since 1990.

The point I am making here is that I believe that negotiating skills are skills that we can all develop. They are not necessarily skills that we are born with. Something that I have noticed over the last 25 years is that the skills necessary to be a successful negotiator today are not the same as they were 25 years ago. They have changed!

Today INTEGRITY is the real key to successful negotiating. In a world where our success is increasingly being determined by the quality of our relationships, win/lose negotiating is out and win/win is the only way! This is the decade of integrity. The skills you'll discover in this book will help in both your personal and professional life as you find yourself —

NEGOTIATING in the Age of INTEGRITY.

Wayne Berry

Introduction

Why Most People Become Shark Bait in Negotiations

After more than 25 years in business I'm convinced that in our western culture, the average person knows very little about negotiating.

If they taught it in school, then I missed it! If they teach it at university, again I see little evidence of it amongst the graduates whom I encounter in business.

I'm convinced also that in our western culture, negotiating skills do not come naturally. What does come naturally, in most negotiating situations, is probably the worst thing that most of us can do, and results in most cases in us becoming **shark bait!**

Let me give you some examples of what I mean.

My wife, Wendy, was shopping recently with a girl friend. Carol wanted to go to the local market to get some bargains and soak up a little of the "culture".

Markets are good fun for practising negotiating skills, too, by the way.

Carol spotted something she really liked for Wendy and wanted her to buy it. Without stopping to think, she encouraged Wendy to try it on.

Then in a voice which could be heard across the other side of the market she said: "Oh it looks great Wendy. It suits you perfectly. You've got to have it. Let's buy it! Buy it!"

Carol was being her enthusiastic self. Isn't this what most people do instinctively when they see something they like? Wendy noticed the stall-owner's face light up as he heard

Carol's words. He started to move towards them, sensing another sale.

"How much is it?" Wendy asked, trying to slow things down a bit, but Carol wasn't going to be slowed down.

"What does it matter? You can afford it!" And then Carol whispered in Wendy's ear: 'Besides it's perfect, and I want you to have it. I'll buy it for you!"

The price probably just went up by ten per cent in the stall-owner's mind. He plucked a price out of the air, $380, and asked if they'd like it in a bag.

Before Wendy could say anything Carol jumped in. And what do you think she said? What would you have said? What would the average person have said?

"That's not bad!" was Carol's response.

In fact, Carol later admitted that it was much more than she had really expected, but like most people, to back down would have caused some embarrassment, and besides, nobody likes anyone else to think that they can't afford something when they're shopping.

Now Wendy who is a keen negotiator, turned to Carol and said: "It's nice, but I'm not sure. It seems a little expensive to me!"

Secretly Wendy was saying to herself: "Whoopee, this is terrific. Great value. I've got to have it! Wow!" But on the surface she was cool. She looked in her wallet and said: "Besides, I've only got $350. Would you take $350 cash for it?"

Now before the stall-owner had a chance to respond, it was Carol to the rescue.

"You've got your credit cards Wendy, don't forget your credit cards!"

"No I left them in the car!" Wendy insisted, as she tucked them out of sight in her purse.

"Don't worry! Here, I'll loan you the $30!" and with this, Carol thrust $50 at Wendy.

So what's the big deal here?

It was a $380 coat. That was a fair price. Carol really didn't understand what Wendy was trying to do. Carol was responding in a perfectly natural and instinctive manner, and if you think that I'm wrong in suggesting that her response was fairly typical of most people, listen around next time you're shopping. Perhaps even listen to yourself.

Counter Instinctive Behaviour

So what am I suggesting?

I'm suggesting that good negotiating skills do not involve *instinctive* behaviour and *instinctive* responses. Rather, our studies of top negotiators have shown that the behaviour that they use to create the outcomes they most desire, are often *counter instinctive* behaviours, *counter instinctive* responses. That is, doing the *opposite* to what comes naturally.

Let's go back to that shopping situation with Carol and Wendy again. How might this situation have unfolded if Carol had acted in a counter instinctive manner?

If, instead of displaying enthusiasm, Carol had behaved in a cool manner towards her intended purchase.

"Look, Wendy, another one of those coats. There are so many around just like this one, and they are all so cheap. I wonder how much this one is?"

Might this have immediately lowered the starting price? Remember that in this case, these two prospective customers may be only seconds from walking away never to be seen again. And when the stall-owner gave her a price, regardless of how good she might have thought it was, what if her response had been:

"How much! You'll have to do better than that!"

Might this also have evoked a response of an even better price? And all of this before the real negotiating had even started.

Then might he have accepted even $30 less, if it appeared to be a take-it-or-leave-it situation?

In similar real life case studies which we have conducted and recorded, we know that the answer in the above three cases, and in more than 60 per cent of cases, very definitely is yes.

So acting in a counter instinctive manner can really pay dividends in negotiating. In this book we'll be looking at how counter instinctive negotiating techniques really work — and *why* they work.

Manipulation

By the way, an issue which sometimes comes up early in my workshops, and maybe it has occurred to you already, is what is the morality, or ethics of using such techniques? Could this be considered manipulation? Am I suggesting that using such techniques mentioned already is the right thing to do?

Well it depends on what your desired outcome is.

Is possessing the knowledge, skills and techniques to be highly manipulative when dealing with others really moral?

Let's tackle this up front. Firstly, let's consider this word, *manipulative*. When I looked in a dictionary to discover the real meaning of this word I was surprised at what I found. It said, and I quote: "Manipulative: To handle skilfully."

So that brings up a question: Is it desirable to be able to handle people and situations skilfully in business and in our personal lives to create the preferred outcomes?

I say it's far more desirable than handling people and situations *unskilfully*, and possibly creating unknown and undesirable outcomes.

I see people doing this almost every day and they create some incredible disasters.

Then there is the question of what is a desirable outcome? Desirable for whom?

Well, we'll be looking later at how to create win/win outcomes, so if that's your desire, I promise you'll be feeling good about what I'm going to suggest later on. However, in the end it's going to come down to how *you* define a desirable outcome and not what I think.

You see in this book, you'll discover some powerful techniques and you'll end up with some powerful tools to work with. But like any tools, they can be used for either good or for evil.

For example, a pen is a tool. Is it in itself good or bad?

Isn't it true that in the hand of someone who knows what he is doing, that a pen can be used to write poetry or a book to inspire future generations? Isn't it equally true that it can be used to mortally wound a person if it were plunged with force into the appropriate part of the human body.

Intrinsically, the pen is neither good nor bad. It's simply a tool. So it is with the techniques that you'll discover in this book. Ultimately, it will be up to you and your integrity as to how you use them.

By the way, many of these are tools which, right now, are probably being used unmercifully upon you. Wouldn't it be a good idea to be aware of them, so you know what's happening and you can protect yourself and those you care about, from their use? I believe so!

Part One

Characteristics of TOP GUN®
Negotiators

Through our TOP GUN® Business Academy and by using Neuro Linguistic Programming (NLP), particularly around behavioural modeling, we've noticed that all top negotiators have certain characteristics in common. There are some things that they *all* do, certain ways of thinking too, which allow them to create predictable and consistent outcomes in their negotiations every time.

You see the question is, if these characteristics and skills have made other people successful, could they make you more successful? The answer, of course, is yes!

So let's take a look at these characteristics of what I like to call TOP GUN negotiators.

I'd like to start by asking the question:

What is negotiating?

I was speaking with a friend on the telephone recently and heard her say: "Well, I really don't negotiate much."

I think that this is a common misconception made by many people who really don't understand what negotiating is. You see, if you don't understand what negotiating is, how can you even know if you are involved in a negotiation? And if you don't know you are even involved in a negotiation, you could lose, not even realising that there may have been another outcome more favourable to you.

For example, I recently took out some life insurance and some income protection cover. Now, because I'm a pilot and I fly small sports aircraft, the insurance company decided that they wanted to attach a special condition to my policy. Basically, it said that they would not pay out on any condition that resulted as a "direct or indirect consequence of engaging in any form of aviation". They sent me a form and asked me to sign and return it.

Wendy handed it to me with the instructions, "Sign here!"

I looked at it and said, "No!"

She gave me that why-are-you-being-so-difficult look, until I explained that here we have a negotiation about to take place. I dare say that many people would have just signed it and mailed it back. After all, it's in writing. It's from a big company which has standard policies and procedures, and it is "not negotiable"! Or is it?

You see someone, somewhere had thought up those words "as a direct or indirect consequence of engaging in any form of aviation", which naturally were designed to favour the insurance company.

If I'd signed without negotiating, think how open-ended that phrase is, "direct and indirect consequence". So, if I was driving to an airport to take a commercial flight out to somewhere and I was involved in a car accident, would that be considered a direct or indirect consequence of engaging in any form of aviation? I suspect that a court of law would rule that is was, and the insurance company would have every right not to pay out. I could have signed my rights away without so much as a second thought.

So began a negotiation to change the wording. Also if they were going to offer me less cover, shouldn't I expect, therefore, that my premium would be lower? Or if this company wouldn't agree to the changes, might there be alternative companies that would agree? There were other possibilities.

I believe that we are surrounded every day by negotiating situations and most people don't even see them.

I also believe that everyone negotiates!

I don't care whether you're in business, in sales, in a relationship or you're a parent. Everyone negotiates! How well you negotiate will determine a great deal of the enjoyment, and/or the pain, that you have in your life.

You see, every time you interact with another human being, and as a result of that interaction some action is taken by either you or that other person — or perhaps by both of you — a negotiation has just taken place.

It could be as simple as asking "Would you mind turning off that light for me", and having that person take that action for you. Or it could be as complex as talking with someone about the sale of a piece of real estate or a motor vehicle. The truth is we all negotiate every day of our lives.

A negotiation takes place whenever you want something from someone, or they want something from you.

As Roger Dawson puts it: "have you noticed how everything you want in this world is already owned or controlled by someone else?"

How effectively this negotiating process occurs will be determined by the skills you have. So there we have it:

Top Gun Negotiator Characteristic # 1

They understand that we all negotiate every
day of our lives.

Let's look at the second characteristic of a Top Gun negotiator, and as we do, let me ask you a question: Is negotiating only about getting what we want in life?

Imagine, if you will, what would happen if we went through life only being concerned about fulfilling *our* needs, *our* wants? What would happen?

Perhaps you may even know people like this? People who do try to operate this way? What happens? How successful are they? What are their relationships like? Are they able to get what they want with total disregard for other people?

Or do they experience conflict, poor relationships with others, and constant frustration? It's one way to live, but what a way to live!

We all know there are more successful strategies for living our life and getting what we want. It's often called, "give and take" isn't it? Sometimes we have to give a little to get what we want in life, and so it is in successful negotiating.

Top Gun negotiators really understand the power of this. They realise that successful negotiating is not just possessing the skills to get what we want. It's also having the skills to facilitate a process which enables other people to get what they want too.

Today more than ever before, success in business is being built on our ability to develop and maintain long term relationships; relationships with clients, suppliers, banks, the people we work with, and so on.

The greedy 1980s was a decade of throw-away relationships, throw-away people, short term profits and exploitation for many business people, and we all know where that has lead many of them — into financial and personal disaster!

In our personal relationships, too, for them to be successful and long term, we know that it's not enough to just satisfy our *own* needs, we have to care about satisfying the other person's needs too, and create good feelings. After all, relationships are more about how people feel than anything else, aren't they?

So, successful negotiating in my opinion must involve skills to communicate in such a way with other people that we enable them to get what *they* want, while we get what *we* want. My friend, Dr Denis Waitley, author of the book, *The Psychology Of Winning*, would call that creating "win/win". For some people this is *counter instinctive* thinking. For others it's not.

So that's:

Top Gun Negotiator Characteristic # 2

They realise that negotiating is not just about the bottom line. It's about the whole process — about building long term relationships, helping other people to get what they want while we get what we want.

.... although it doesn't have to be!

Have you noticed that?

Some people, under certain circumstances, do not care about the long term relationship. There are some sharks out there, and if you don't have good negotiating skills you can very quickly become... shark bait.

Top Gun Negotiator Characteristic # 3

They understand the structure of negotiating

We've noticed that all successful negotiators have a certain structure to their process of negotiating — a process of *interaction* and *communication which works for them*. So they get what they want more often. We've also noticed that they are able to create outcomes where the person they are negotiating with, feels that he got what he wanted too. It's a structure which exists whether you realise it or not.

The difference between a skilled and an unskilled negotiator is that the skilled negotiator understands the structure and recognises the stages of the negotiation. He or she understands what is happening throughout the negotiating process and is empowered by this.

The unskilled negotiator doesn't understand the process. As a consequence he doesn't know where he is at for most of the negotiating process and he often feels out of control, and disempowered by this lack of understanding.

It's like playing a game where you don't know the rules. If you don't know the rules, how would you even know when the game has begun, or when it has reached its mid point or is nearing its conclusion.

It's like baking a cake without the recipe.

If you didn't know to beat the eggs before placing the cake in the oven, you might just end up with egg on your face, right? And so it is with negotiating.

I remember a negotiation many years ago involving some office space. The person I was negotiating with gave me a deadline for when he wanted a decision from me.

He said he had another prospective tenant and he wouldn't budge on the lease figure. He also said if I didn't want it the other people probably would.

I panicked at the thought of losing this ideal property as I'd spent so much time looking around already. The point is, I thought we were at the end of the negotiation and I conceded to his requests.

In retrospect, now that I have a better understanding of the process and stages of negotiating, I can see that in reality, we were nowhere near the end.

Indeed, we were just about to start the real negotiating. Not realising this cost me a great deal of money.

By the way, if you're in sales you'll know that there are certain steps of the sale, aren't there? If, for example, you try to close the sale before you've understood your client's needs, it's highly unlikely that you'll end up with a sale.

Successful negotiating is exactly the same but the steps of negotiating ARE NOT the same as the steps in selling.

I see sales people every day who think that because they understand selling this makes them great negotiators. It doesn't! I see them become shark bait when dealing with even unskilled negotiators, before they even know what's happened.

So later on, we'll be looking at this structure, and the stages of negotiating, in detail.

Top Gun Negotiator Characteristic # 4
They know how to create a real win/win outcome
where both parties feel that they won.

Characteristic #2, we said, involved building long term relationships and helping other people get what they want while we get what we want. This is commonly known as creating win/win.

Almost everyone today has heard of this term, but I'm convinced that although most people are familiar with it, very few people really understand it. Even fewer know how to create it.

So for me, a win/win outcome in a negotiation is more than just helping other people get what they want while we get what we want. That's only half the definition.

For me, real win/win is created when we help another person to get what they want, while we get what we want, and where ***both parties feel that they won.***

Again, it's not just about the bottom line. It's about the process — and this process involves people's feelings.

Years ago I was negotiating a lease on some other office space. I got it, too, for less than what I wanted to pay — far less — and for far less than what they had originally asked for. But despite this, I didn't feel that I'd really won.

The person I was negotiating with had not created a win/win outcome. He'd come very close, mind you, but in the end he blew it. In fact, in the end I felt that I'd lost, even though the bottom line dollars were better then my original expectation.

How could that be and what were the consequences?

Well, the person I was dealing with could have done business with me many times again afterwards, had he created a real win/win, where *I* felt good about the outcome. But he didn't. I can vividly remember that "ripped off" feeling even to this day. Although I have seen him many times since then and could have often used and recommended his services, I haven't, and I'm sure he has no idea why not.

So what happened?

Well, after we had concluded negotiations and the papers had been signed, he revealed that the owner of the property had authorised him to offer me a six month rent-free period, as well as the lower rental rate we'd finally agreed on.

He thought it was a great joke and an example of what a superb negotiator he really was. The reverse was really true and he didn't understand the damage he'd just done to our on-going relationship. It was a classic example of how to create something which is not win/win.

Good feelings by both parties are so important to creating win/win. If he had remained silent, I never would have known and I would have felt that I really had won too. That's the hallmark of a true win/win negotiator.

This is also a good example of how some highly competitive people do respond instinctively during negotiations. But good negotiating often involves counter instinctive behaviour. This is another example of how responding in a counter instinctive manner would have created a more desirable outcome.

Top Gun Negotiator Characteristic # 5
Top Gun negotiators feel good about negotiating
and look for opportunities to negotiate.

In my workshops we often talk about how most people feel about negotiating, and we've discovered that many people don't feel good about negotiating at all.

So let me ask you that question: how do you really feel about negotiating?

It's a funny thing, but in our western society we instinctively tend to avoid negotiating. Let me give you an example.

You're buying an electrical appliance, say a CD player. The price-tag says, *"Special. Was $650. Now $450".*

The average person, (and I know this is true because we've surveyed it) will either take it or leave it. If they think it's a good deal, they'll most likely pay the $450 and feel they got a "bargain".

Let's shift this scene to Hong Kong — same situation, but this time you're a resident of Hong Kong. This is where you grew up. What do you do? Do you pay $450? I bet you don't, because in that city, in that culture, you know that the price-tag is just the opening position for a negotiation.

It's just somewhere to start — and so the game begins — and it's highly unlikely that you will pay the price on the tag. Why is that? It's cultural conditioning.

For some reason many people in our culture don't believe it's "nice" to negotiate, so they don't.

So, what happens when someone from an eastern culture comes to live or visit here. Have you ever done business with someone like this. They negotiate and save money in almost every situation. They're very keen and often very successful business people, and because many of the people they're doing business with here are not practised negotiators, they do particularly well. And good luck to them too.

See, if you were walking down a country lane and you came across a $100 note lying there and there was nobody about, there was no way of finding the owner, would you bend down and pick it up?

Well, I'm not sure about you but I would!

Negotiating is a little like walking down the country road of life. Every day you will come across opportunities to negotiate. If, because of your cultural conditioning or other negative feelings that you have about negotiating, you pass these opportunities by, you'll leave money and other benefits lying wasted on the road behind you, and that would be such a shame, wouldn't you agree?

If you don't believe me, try this exercise that I give participants of our TOP GUN® Master Negotiator Workshop, after just their first evening with us.

I challenge them to open their eyes for one week and look for opportunities to negotiate, where normally they would not. I challenge them to step outside their cultural conditioning, for just one week, and to keep score of the savings they make, or the improved financial situations they negotiate. The success stories are sometimes quite amazing. I've had people save many times the fee they invested to do our five week course, in just this one week.

Top Gun Negotiator Characteristic # 6
They do not seek total approval from the other party, for being liked or for being totally reasonable.

Another reason why many people don't negotiate more often is because of fear of rejection.

They have an overwhelming desire not to make waves, to be totally likeable at all times and to be totally reasonable at all times.

Well, sure, I can understand this. It's great to be liked and because of self-esteem many people need the approval of others to feel good about themselves. And yes, it's better to be liked than disliked. But in negotiating, this instinctive level of desire can be so high, that it can be fatal, and we can become shark bait.

Some people intuitively want to be liked so much, that they won't put forward what they really want out of the negotiation.

They are so afraid of being seen as unreasonable, that they don't say what's on their mind. Instead, when the other party puts forward their requests or demands, again not wanting to be seen as unreasonable, they sometimes concede to these requests, without so much as a word.

Doing so can build internal resentment, and we can end up feeling bad about the negotiation, and that's not win/win.

Top Gun Negotiator Characteristic # 7
They are provokable and unpredictable.

They are fair, but not totally reasonable all of the time.

You see, if you were totally reasonable all of the time, seeking to be a "nice person" all of the time, and always avoiding confrontation, guess what that would make you?

It would make you totally predictable and totally unprovokable.

So, if you were totally predictable all of the time (because you're a nice person) and the other person knew that no matter what they demanded, or how they behaved, you would always respond the same nice way, would that make you just a little bit vulnerable in a negotiation?

Think about it!

Have you seen people taken advantage of in life simply because they were known to be "nice"?

I certainly have. Indeed, I've been that person and I've become shark bait.

In 1987 in my seminar promotions business, I had a distributor in a capital city where I didn't have a branch of my own. On a particular promotion featuring a very famous American speaker, this promoter called me to say that he was going to be late with a progress payment. He asked would I mind covering this payment and he would catch up with the next payment.

I felt sorry for him. He was new to the business, struggling a little, but trying hard, so I agreed. I didn't want to disappoint the speaker either. Besides, I knew he'd make it up on the next payment in two weeks time. I paid the US$3,000 for him.

In two weeks time, he was still in trouble, apologetic, and asked if I could cover him again.

I had now set up a situation where I already had a financial interest in the success of the promotion in his city. If he failed, or the seminar didn't go ahead, I stood to lose the US$3,000 I'd already put up. Besides, what would I say to the speaker who trusted me to protect his interests? He promised me he'd make it up to me on the day of the seminar, when the final monies were in. Wanting to be reasonable and helpful, I once again agreed.

The week of the seminar came and it was time for this promoter to send me about $15,000 for stocks of the speaker's tape programmes which would be sold on the day. Surprise, surprise he claimed, again, not to have the money. Could I possibly ship the tapes, and he'd pay me out of the sales on the day? After all, I'd be there to see that it all went well.

I considered my options.

If the tapes weren't shipped, there would be no tape sales, clients would miss out, so would the speaker, and so would the promoter. Like the nice guy I was, I agreed.

Can you see what I was doing to myself here?

I had become totally *predictable* and totally *unprovokable*.

As one totally unreasonable request after another was granted, he became even more confident, even more certain that I would say yes to the next one. And he was right. I did. Instead of making him responsible for solving his own problems, I had bought into his problem and soon owned it.

This predictability and lack of provokability, ended up costing me more than $50,000 on this one occasion alone. And I'd like to tell you that I learnt from it, but the truth is I didn't. Not at the time anyway. I repeated this mistake many times over, until by 1990, this response, which was an intuitive response for me, had cost me more than $300,000. Whew! What a price to pay to learn this lesson.

Today, I'm somewhat more provokable and much less predictable.

Top Gun Negotiator Characteristic # 8
They have the confidence which comes from having developed the skills to be good at negotiating.

I believe that much of a person's fear of negotiating comes from a lack of confidence brought about by a lack of skills. Improve the skills, your confidence level goes up, fears diminish and thus begins a "reframe" (as we call it in NLP terms), of how we see negotiating.

If we see negotiating as something which is unpleasant or something we are not good at, then naturally we will avoid negotiating, and this can be very costly.

So, in this book you're going to have an opportunity to develop some skills that will make you more confident and this is the eighth characteristic of a top negotiator.

They've taken the time to develop the skills and they keep the skills updated continually by studying negotiating. They attend the courses and they practise these skills all the time, in real life negotiating situations, every day.

Top Gun Negotiator Characteristic # 9
Top Gun negotiators understand that negotiating is just a game, and because it's just a game, they don't take it too seriously. They enjoy the game and as a consequence it's fun and more rewarding.

On the subject of confidence, and our attitude towards negotiating, I'm going to suggest that you totally reframe the way you see negotiating.

I'm going to suggest that from this day on, you see every negotiating situation as simply another opportunity to play the game — the negotiating game.

That's right, and like all games, the game of negotiating can be fun. And again like all games, the more skilled you are and the more you understand the rules of the game, the more fun it can be.

Think about it. Isn't this the secret of success for many famous professional athletes, golfers, tennis players and the like? And isn't it also true, that when they take the game too seriously, take themselves too seriously, this is when their game goes "off" and they experience the anxiety which comes from trying too hard? The consequences can be disastrous and so it is, too, with negotiating.

The moment it becomes more than a game, is the moment you are in serious jeopardy of losing your cool, and losing it all.

These days, I often negotiate for friends, just for the fun.

Top Gun Negotiator Characteristic # 10
They believe that everything is negotiable.

It is my unshakeable belief that *everything is negotiable.*

That's right — *everything!*

Does this mean you should negotiate on everything? Well why not? By the way, as we'll discover more later on, our beliefs tend to shape our reality.

But, did I hear you say, some things simply *aren't* negotiable?

Many years ago now I helped a friend shop for a dining suite. We went to a large and very well known department store. He found the one he wanted and it had a price-tag on it of $2,100.

I recognised immediately that it was several hundred dollars above his intended budget.

When I pointed this out to him he said: "Don't worry, I don't intend to pay $2,100 for it, I can get it for much less than that."

I said: "No way, not here. This a department store they won't discount it for you. This is the price, right here on the sticker."

Isn't it funny, how when it's in writing, instinctively we think that the price is set in concrete? (We'll talk more about this later on.)

Then I watched in awe as he successfully negotiated a discount. He did get it for what he wanted to pay. It was a major lesson for me.

Now, I'm not saying that you'll always get a price reduction, but I am suggesting that everything is negotiable.

For example, if he hadn't negotiated a discount, could my friend have negotiated free delivery or an accessory thrown in? Or a variation of the terms of payment?

These are all negotiable! Everything is negotiable — particularly when you've got the skills.

Top Gun Negotiator Characteristic # 11
They have learnt to use counter instinctive thinking and responses in negotiating situations.

Something that I have really noticed with all top negotiators is that they do not respond or react in negotiating situations like the average person.

Indeed, their reaction is often directly opposite to the way the average person would react.

So the point I am making here is that Top Gun negotiators understand the power of responding in a counter instinctive manner in negotiating situations.

That is, they understand that the response which works best is usually directly opposite to that which our normal instinctive response would be. I spoke about this earlier, and we'll be looking at the power of this characteristic all the way through this book.

Top Gun Negotiator Characteristic # 12
They understand that they are dealing with people
not companies, and that these people have needs,
emotions, and egos. Negotiating is a process of
satisfying these personal needs.

If you're involved in business negotiations, who do you negotiate with? When I ask my seminar audiences I sometimes get a list of companies, but that's a big mistake. We really don't negotiate with companies and organisations, do we? Negotiations always involve interacting and communicating with *people.*

Remember, in business negotiating, you are negotiating with people, not companies. These people may be representing companies, but they are still people — people who all have emotions, egos, and feelings, and it's important to realise that humans are creatures of emotion, not simply of logic.

You may be negotiating business issues, but a great deal of how the person you're negotiating with sees these issues will be determined by their personal motivations, their own perception filters, their own model of the world, their emotions.

In my early days in business, I used to feel intimidated negotiating with large companies. This is a fairly natural and instinctive response, wouldn't you agree? I felt inadequate. This large organisation, so big, so powerful, me on the other hand, so small, so unimportant by comparison. Finally, experience showed me that the people who represented these large organisations were just people. People just like me, with insecurities and with personal interests in the outcome of the negotiation, just like me.

This realisation completely reframed the way I saw negotiations and empowered me to be more effective in my negotiations.

NEGOTIATING in the Age of INTEGRITY

Top Gun Negotiator Characteristic # 13

They look beyond the requests and demands of the other party and seek to understand their intention, their real motive. Then they seek to meet this dominant, often hidden, need.

It's important to understand that the major driving force behind all requests made in every negotiation is the desire of the other person to satisfy a human need, and this need is linked to their human value system.

Of course, what's important to one person may not be of importance to another person, because their basic value systems may be different. That's why it's always important to look *behind* a person's request in a negotiation, to seek to understand their *intention*, the real needs which they are seeking to fulfil.

If we look only at their requests — their demands — we may not be able to agree to these requests. However, if we look at their *intention* — the real motive behind their demands — there may be any number of ways of satisfying these underlying needs and fulfilling their intentions.

For example, in 1992, one of the key people in our organisation asked for a substantial increase in salary. Frankly, we weren't in a position at that time to meet that request. We had capped our overheads for that year, a year of deep recession.

However, this person really needed an increase and deserved it too.

So what would the normal instinctive response of the average negotiator be in this situation?

I suspect they might have politely explained that an increase now was not possible. If the member of staff had persisted, the situation may have hotted up, perhaps even ended in bad feeling or a resignation. This would have been a real lose/lose outcome.

However, remembering that good negotiating is counter instinctive — responding in the opposite manner to what is natural, and remembering that people are always motivated by deeper issues than those which are revealed in their initial request, I decided to see if there was some other way of meeting Jane's need.

So I asked the question: 'Why now Jane? What has changed to create this need all of a sudden?"

What would she use this increase for? (We'll talk later about this important phase of every negotiation, where we gather information.)

Of course, Jane could have told me to mind my own business, but we were both intent on creating win/win. So I sat and listened, while Jane explained that the car she was driving, was driving her crazy. She needed to replace it quickly, and she felt that she deserved a new car too. That meant financing this purchase.

So now I understood the *intention* behind Jane's request.

That put a whole new light on the situation, and within hours, we were able to satisfy Jane's need, allowing her to move into a shiny near-new red sports car, without even committing to a finance company, while satisfying my need not to increase our overheads. How?

I had such a vehicle that I hardly ever drove.

It had been sitting in my garage for weeks on end without being used. I favoured another bigger vehicle that the company had. It was costing me substantial dollars in a monthly lease to have this car sit idle and this was such a waste. Jane drove that car for two years until the lease ran out. A beautiful example of win/win, all because I responded in a counter instinctive manner and looked behind her request to her intention, her need.

> ## Top Gun Negotiator Characteristic # 14
> They understand the importance of being totally present and totally focused while negotiating.

In our Top Gun workshops we have a saying: "the point of power is in the present."

Amongst other things, this is a reminder that we need to focus on what we're doing at the time we're doing it. For example, when I'm flying my plane I sometimes don't hear some of my passengers' chatter. I'm totally focused on all aspects of what I'm doing in safely flying that plane, monitoring all systems, keeping an eye out for air traffic.

What if I took my focus off of these critical areas, even for a minute? Well, I could crash and burn!

It's a little like that in a negotiation too. We need to concentrate wholly on what is happening in the present, or we might overlook something, and crash and burn.

I was sitting in on a negotiation with a client a few years ago and heard the other party make a remark about a 3¢ increase in the cost of a particular item being used in the construction of an office building. It was mentioned quickly, as part of a larger, seemingly more important, issue involving tens of thousands of dollars which was being discussed. I could see that my client's mind was on this bigger issue and I wasn't sure he was paying attention, as by saying nothing, he'd just agreed to this 3¢ increase.

I asked if I could question this 3¢ increase and suddenly my client realised why.

With some simple maths, it was clear that because of the number of these items involved, he had nearly let a $7,500 increase get by — totally unchallenged.

My good friend, American motivational speaker E. James Rohn has a great phrase to remind us of the importance of staying focused. He says: "Wherever you are *be there!*"

It can be costly to have an out-of-body experience when you really should have been there. Always focus on what's happening and if you need to, ask for the pace to be slowed down. Ask for clarification.

Top Gun Negotiator Characteristic # 15

They exercise full sensory acuity during negotiations, looking at the body language and other non-verbal cues, to gain a fuller understanding of what is really happening.

Many studies have been done into human communication over the last 20 years. They have all concluded that verbal communication accounts for only about 7 per cent of the total communication process.

That leaves a massive 93 per cent which is not verbal.

A friend of mine, Australian author and speaker Alan Pease, says that at least 70 per cent of this 93 per cent is body language.

The remaining 23 per cent is not verbal or body language. It is a level of communication which goes beyond the physical. Again, exhaustive studies have concluded that we human beings communicate at a much deeper level than most of us are aware.

Many books have been written on this subject and the science of understanding this level of communication is known as "Sentics". I don't propose to go into an in-depth explanation of what this is. Suffice to say that human communication is much more than what we *say*.

Sometimes, it's just as important *how* something is said — the body language, the tonality of the voice, etc. — as much as *what* is said.

Often, too, it's not so much what *is* said, as what is *not* said. We'll talk more about this later on.

However, sensory acuity is something which can be developed with practice. It's simply being more aware of what you notice — what you see, what you hear, what you feel. It's an important skill to develop.

Top Gun Negotiator Characteristic # 16

They know what they want before they start negotiating —
or at least have a fairly good idea.

If you were setting out on a journey, what's the first thing you would decide on? Let's say it was a holiday?

Wouldn't you decide on your destination first?

Once you had chosen your destination, wouldn't this then enable you to work backwards from there, to decide on the best way to get there?

Isn't it just as important in a negotiation for you to have some idea of your desired destination before you set out?

If you didn't, then wherever you happened to arrive at would probably be good enough, even if it was somebody else's destination.

It's important not to close off options or be too singleminded in negotiating, but it's just as important to know what your ideal outcome would be, *before* you get started.

I've seen too many people begin negotiating without having any real idea of where they wanted to take the negotiation. As a consequence they've arrived at an agreement which was not in their best interest.

In negotiating — and in life — if you don't have a plan of your own you'll soon become a part of someone else's plan. Good negotiators know this and use this.

I've seen employees with no idea of what they wanted, go into an annual salary or performance review without any objectives. They come out with a horizontal shift within their company, or a transfer to another location where they didn't really want to go, or a reduction in real terms in their income and other benefits, all because they had no idea of what they really wanted, and because the other person did.

So be aware of the danger of being what I like to call, a "wandering generality" in a negotiation.

Top Gun Negotiator Characteristic # 17
They always know their bottom line before they start
negotiating.

I have a saying that I like to run my businesses by, that is: "unprofitable business has no place in business at all."

What I mean by this is that I will not seek to do business "at any costs" any more.

Have you ever been in a negotiating situation where, because of the amount of time and effort you've invested, you have decided to get that business, no matter how low you had to go? I've seen people do exactly that with diabolical consequences.

In the mid 1980s, my seminar business operated a division known as The Australian Business Network. Members would pay an annual membership fee to attend all seminars, workshops, special events, etc. and also receive other special "members only" benefits. It was like a season ticket and the value was tremendous. You received more than $3,000 worth of benefits for a $1,000 up-front fee. It benefited my business too — these members were paying 12 months in advance and this was great for cash flow.

One of my distributors in another capital city decided to emulate the system in his city, so he renamed it, and started selling memberships.

Soon after this, he started a negotiation with a large company in his city which liked the system and wanted to take out more than 100 memberships. For this volume, they wanted a discount. In fact, they asked for half price. Now, it was already a highly discounted product but my distributor was impressed by the numbers. He fought hard to lessen the discount, but in the end, accepted it. The client was so happy that not only did he take the initial 100, each month he added more.

The people who were buying these super cheap memberships were the people who used to come to this distributor's seminars every time and pay full price. Before too long, his volume of regular priced tickets had dropped off alarmingly. So much so, that his business was no longer profitable.

He went to his accountant for advice. When he did the figures, he discovered that each membership he was selling at this low price, was costing him $100 *more* to deliver over the 12 months, than he was receiving. In other words, the more he sold, the more he lost. What a situation to be in!

The mistake he made was not knowing his bottom line before he started negotiating. Had he done this exercise beforehand, he would never have agreed to a 50 per cent discount on an already highly discounted product. Instead, he flew by the seat of his pants, thought it looked good, and in the end, he was in big trouble.

A professional negotiator always knows his or her bottom line before the start of the negotiation.

This bottom line is the point at which it's no longer OK to continue negotiating. This is when it is wiser to simply walk away from the deal.

By the way, this isn't always a dollar-related issue. It could relate to how the other party is playing the game.

If, for example, your bottom line is that certain behaviour, certain treatment by the other party towards you — like bullying tactics, bad language, overtly expressed anger, etc. — is not OK, then it's important that you know how far you are prepared to let them go, before you either walk away or tell them that you will, if such behaviour continues.

I've walked away from such situations which were serving no purpose, but making me feel bad, and where I wasn't prepared to put up with it any longer, only to find that I was immediately invited back, and the behaviour which I found unacceptable was dropped.

Notice I didn't say *bad* behaviour because that would be a judgement from my model of the world. However, I have a right not to be around behaviour that goes against my own integrity and you have the right to draw just such a line, in every negotiation. Use it and don't be used.

So there you have it, 17 key characteristics of all Top Gun negotiators. Certainly there are more. These are the ones at the top of my list, and we'll deal with the other minor characteristics, later in this book. Also we'll be looking at:

1. The structure of negotiating

2. Sources of power in negotiations

3. Tactics, ploys, gambits and dirty tricks that you are likely to encounter in negotiations

4. Some guidelines or rules of successful negotiating

5. Some of the common mistakes made in negotiations and how to avoid them.

Part Two

The Counter Instinctive Model of Negotiating

The Structure of Negotiating

I mentioned earlier, that I've noticed all successful negotiators have a certain structure to their process of negotiating. Indeed, there are certain phases that we go through in every negotiation, regardless of what it is that we are negotiating.

In a big negotiation, some of these phases could take days, weeks, months or even years. In smaller negotiations like, say, buying an ice-cream, some of these phases can be over in a millisecond.

Understanding what these phases are, will empower you.

Not understanding the process or stages of negotiating, can often lead to a feeling of being out of control and disempowered.

So, here are the stages or phases that we have identified as being significant. We will include them in our model — our Counter Instinctive Model of Negotiating.

There are six stages in this model:

1. The PREPARATION Phase — Preparing for the negotiation.
2. The RAPPORT Phase — Beginning to interact with the other party.
3. The GATHERING OF INFORMATION Phase — Ascertaining what the other party might want.
4. The PROBING AND EXPLORING OPTIONS Phase — Exploring the options available, sometimes

discovering how flexible or inflexible the other party is, and maybe even establishing the possible range of the negotiation. (That is, how high and how low they may or may not go.)

5. The BARTERING/TRADING CONCESSIONS Phase — "Wheeling and dealing" and sometimes giving and asking for concessions.

6. The FINALISING OR NAILING DOWN Phase — Finalising the agreement — who will do what, when, where, and how? This is where we confirm the agreement and where we consider what can be done if either, or both parties, break any agreements made.

This part of the book looks at each of these phases in detail, and shows how they all play a part in the success or lack of success, of any negotiation.

Not only is each phase important, the order in which they are listed is important as well. Like the steps or rungs on a ladder, miss a step and you may be at risk of taking a tumble. Miss two steps and you and the other party may come crashing down to earth with a thud!

For example, if you move to Phase 3 — the Gathering of Information Phase — and begin seeking this information from the other party without first establishing some rapport — Phase 2 — you may be told to get lost!

If you try to move to the Bartering Phase without first building some rapport and without first probing for and exploring some options, you may find that you are way off target with what you are offering. You may offer too much or not enough. You may give up some items too quickly that you should have held back.

It's important to take the process one step at a time, and if it's needed, sometimes quite slowly. In our western culture, however, where we are used to instant coffee, fast communication and instant gratification, there is a tendency to "bottom line" negotiations too quickly.

Again our philosophy of Counter Instinctive Negotiating comes into play, realising that if the normal instinctive behaviour of most people in our culture is to "bottom line" a negotiation, probably the best outcomes are produced by not "bottom lining" the negotiation too quickly. Remember negotiating is about the process, not just the bottom line.

Counter Instinctive Negotiating Phase #1
PREPARATION

The preparation phase is vitally important to create the outcomes you desire in your negotiations.

The average person, however, does very little if any preparation. He tends to bowl into the negotiation and say and do things, literally "off the top of his head", and it shows. Against a skilled negotiator, he can very quickly become shark bait!

There's an old saying that: "proper preparation prevents poor performance" and this is especially true in negotiating. So when do we prepare, and how?

Preparation — good preparation — involves the hardest work known to man. It's simple, everyone can do it, but very few people actually do very much of it throughout their lifetime. It's called THINKING! Good preparation involves thinking before acting and it can sometimes occur even before contact is made with the other party.

Working with top negotiators and modelling ourselves on what it is that they do, we've come up with a checklist for preparation. Let's review it here now.

Checklist For Good Preparation:

✓ Know what your own bottom line is

That is, how high am I prepared to go (if I'm buying) or how low am I prepared to go (if I'm selling)? By the way, I don't just mean dollars. Not all negotiations involve dollars. There can be many other factors involved.

We call this bottom line our Lowest Acceptable Position (LAP). As a buyer, this is the highest amount of dollars I'm prepared to spend. This is where I will draw the line. It's simply not worth going above this line. This is the point above which it's not worth negotiating any more.

As a seller, this LAP is the *least* amount that I will accept, or where I will draw the line and decide it's not worth negotiating for less than this. You'll find an illustration of this on the next page. It's amazing, but I find people in the middle of negotiations who have not yet established their bottom line.

If you haven't established your bottom line in advance, you may well get carried away in the heat of the moment, or try to figure it out in your head, and go beyond the point where the outcome of the negotiation is in your best interest.

Knowing where to draw this line will empower you. Not knowing can *dis*empower you, cause you to feel stressed and uncertain, and even have you agreeing to something, which later will seem crazy.

Now the flip side to this "bottom line" issue is:

✓ Clarify your ideal "best scenario" outcome for this negotiation

In negotiating terms, we call this your HAP or your Highest Advanced Position — the *most* you feel you could ask for and get.

As a buyer, this is the *lowest* possible price that you feel you may be able to pay and still get what you want. It's a target to shoot for. If you're a seller, it's the highest possible price that you feel you may be able to ask for — and still get the deal. This is also illustrated in the diagram.

So, now you have established your LAP and your HAP. That is your Lowest Acceptable Position and Highest Advanced Position. This gap in between effectively

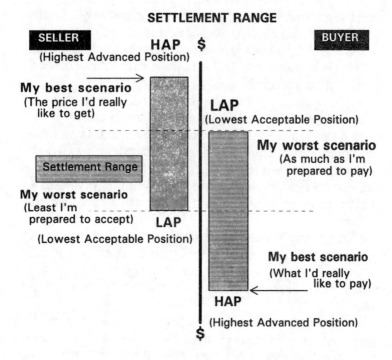

LAP The least you would be willing to accept. Anything lower and you would be better off NOT negotiating!

HAP The most you would ask for and generally the most you could expect.

The Unspoken Rules

1. Keep as close to your HAP as possible and as far away from your LAP as is prudent.

2. Do not let your opponent know your LAP.

3. In ADVANCE determine your FALL BACK POSITION — the concessions you would be prepared to make. Be sure to build in some that you feel would be important to the other party.

4. Keep your expectations (your subconscious intention) high and actively work to lower your opponent's expectations. Use the "flinch".

becomes your Negotiating Range — your high point and your low point.

Now as part of your best scenario position, you need to:

✓ Clarify your real objectives

What do you really want? What are your:

➤ MUST HAVEs — what are the items on your list that you must *absolutely* have. Clarity around this list can really empower you and prevent you from being distracted or side-tracked.

➤ INTEND TO HAVEs — This is a list of items, which in the most ideal scenario you *would like* to have, but they are not absolutely essential.

➤ NICE TO HAVEs — These are items that you feel it would be *nice* to have but in the end are really not critically important to you.

For example, in the early 1990s, I was involved in a negotiation to occupy the top floor of an office building in what was known to be a high rent business district in an Australian capital city.

My MUST HAVEs were that I didn't want to sign a lease which would lock us into the location for say three or five years.

Amongst my INTEND TO HAVEs was the stipulation that, whilst I eventually wanted the entire top floor which was vacant, I didn't want it all right away. I wanted to pay only for what we occupied, which initially was only to be about half, and then pay more as we took more.

Also, I had set what could have been seen to be a fairly unrealistic intention, of paying only $6 to $7 per square foot. In this area it was not unusual to pay $20 to $25 per square foot. However, at this time Australia was deep in recession and vacancies were high. Some landlords were being, shall we say, "flexible".

My NICE TO HAVEs but not essential, included 10 parking spaces in the basement car park, and that the landlord should pay for all partitioning. At the time, the floor was completely open with no partitioning.

✓ **Do your best to anticipate what the other party's objectives might be**

What do they really want? What are their most likely MUST HAVEs, INTEND TO HAVEs, NICE TO HAVEs?

Make up a list. Write them down just as you did with your list. (By the way, considering these questions may give you some idea of the other party's HAP — Highest Advanced Position or best scenario outcome — and the other party's LAP — Lowest Acceptable Position, the worst acceptable scenario for them. In other words, their possible Negotiating Range.)

If you now compare their negotiating range, with your negotiating range and they overlap, we have a possible Settlement Range — an area where both parties may get some of what they want. Not necessarily *all* they want, but *some*. The greater the overlap, the more both parties may be able to get of what they want. This Settlement Range is graphically illustrated in the diagram on page 34 and this terminology will be useful to you later on.

Incidentally, if there is no overlap — no common settlement range — then it may be unlikely that a settlement can be reached until this range is further negotiated. Now, I didn't say impossible — just unlikely. It simply means that until the expectations of one or more of the parties alter, a settlement may not occur ... yet. More negotiating will be required.

(By the way, in the case of my office rental negotiation, I guessed that ideally this landlord would be looking for a lease, and a minimum of $10 to $15 per square foot.)

On his INTEND TO HAVEs list, there was the question of "outgoings", like communal lighting and cleaning, elevator maintenance, etc. This could be another $5 or more per square foot that he might be looking for.

On his NICE TO HAVEs list, I felt fairly sure he would want me to occupy and pay for the entire top floor.

Now it's time to compare our two lists to see...

✓ How far apart are these two objectives?

1. Are they very far apart at all? If so, how much?

2. Where do they overlap or have commonality? Remember that later on, these areas of "common ground" will provide a platform on which to build rapport and a relationship and begin the negotiating. Later on — in NLP terms — we'll be calling this creating an "Agree to Agree" frame.

3. Where are they in conflict?

4. How great is this conflict really?

5. And finally, the big question: how could you create win/win here?

Well, as you can see in my rental negotiation we would probably be a fair distance apart on the per-square-foot-lease figure, and frankly I wanted to pay no outgoings at all. On the other hand, I wanted the space, and he wanted to lease it — at least I assumed this when I spotted his sign on the front of the building. He had chosen to handle the rental or lease himself, rather than use a real estate agent.

✓ Consider what the other party's *intentions* might be, behind any request, or requests, that they may have already given you, or you suspect they want from you

We spoke earlier about how important it is to remember that the major driving force behind all requests made in every negotiation, is the desire of the other person to satisfy one, or a range of human needs.

Now, it's time to put ourselves into the shoes of the other person, and look behind any such requests. What is it that they really want? What is the real need that they would like to satisfy? What is the real intention behind their words.

If we look only at their requests, their demands, we may not be able to agree to these requests. However, if we look behind their words, there may be any number of ways of satisfying these underlying needs.

In NLP terms, this is called doing a "second position shift", where we seek to experience the other person's world, from their perspective, rather than our own.

✓ How can I make them feel like they have won?

Again we spoke earlier about the importance of allowing the other person to feel that they had won in the negotiation. Are we allowing for this in our planning? How can we create this important feeling?

Remember, successful negotiating is not just about the bottom line. It's about feelings, too, and we are all creatures of emotion.

✓ What is your next option if all should fail in this negotiation?

While we don't expect this to happen, having a contingency plan should the negotiation fail, gives us power. Any time we have alternatives we have power. Any time we don't have alternatives, this is when we will most likely feel pressured and stressed, and have a strong emotional attachment to the outcome of the negotiation. This can be very disempowering.

So the question I ask myself is: what's the worst thing that can happen if I don't get what I need here?

Seeking the answers to that question forces us to think about what the real — I stress — REAL consequences would be if the results of this negotiation were not totally in our favour.

Fear of diabolical consequences can be totally disempowering. One of my American friends likes to say that the letters F.E.A.R stand for **F**alse **E**xpectations **A**ppearing **R**eal, and isn't that so true? Very often many of the fears we have are not real, they are imagined.

For example, as time went on when we were negotiating for that office space, my general manager feared that time would run out before we had secured an alternative to the training venue we were using. Each day that passed she became more concerned. I'm sure that in her mind she saw the day when seminar participants would arrive at our old venue, only to find that they were locked out. She saw herself there at the door, embarrassed, explaining why they were locked out, why we hadn't been able to secure another venue. She probably saw people looking disappointed, maybe even angry and she felt stressed out.

How real were these fears?

Weren't there other options?

Although it wouldn't have been our number one choice, we probably could have found another temporary venue for a week or two. We could have even postponed a few training sessions temporarily. The point I'm making, is that there were options. It would not have been the end of the world if we had been forced to walk away from this negotiation empty-handed.

Have a look at the worst possible thing that could happen to you. In most cases, it would not mean the end of your world. You would survive. In even the worst case scenario you probably do have options. Having a known fall back position is very empowering. It removes the fear of the unknown.

✓ Decide what issues you want to cover in the negotiation

Sometimes it's better to hold back certain issues for another time, another negotiation. It can be better to reach a negotiated agreement before raising other matters, too. Timing can be very important.

For example, naming rights for an office building. Let's say we wanted to able to put our TOP GUN sign across the top of the building. Raising this issue as a part of the negotiation could have resulted in a flat NO! Asking for this *after* the negotiation had been concluded, could result in this request being approved very easily. For example:

"Of course, Mr Landlord, this agreement allows for our name across the top of the building too, doesn't it?"

This is called *nibbling*.

Suddenly, when it looks like the negotiation is over, an issue is raised which potentially could undo all the good work done. In most cases, you'll find that the pressure this creates, results in the other party fairly readily agreeing to this last minute request, rather than upsetting the agreement already in place.

We'll talk more about nibbling later on, and what to do if you're on the receiving end of a nibble.

✓ Consider the timetables:

➣ What is your timeframe?

➣ Are there any time pressures from your perspective?

➣ What is the other party's timeframe?

➣ Are there likely to be any time pressures on the other party?

➣ What is the possible impact of these pressures on both sides?

➣ Is there any way of relieving this time pressure on yourself?

➣ Are there any actions which you could take which would either increase or decrease the time pressure on the other party?

This could become a vitally important aspect of the negotiation later on, or even right from the beginning.

In my rental case I did have a deadline. As I mentioned earlier, we needed a new venue for our seminars. We were using a convention centre for our courses in this city and had a separate location for our office. We were bursting at the seams at the office as we were growing quickly at the time, and our rental period had already expired. We were on a month-by-month basis which could be terminated at any time. Also we had a new series of programmes booked to start within a fortnight. Our current venue could not accommodate us and we hadn't yet found an alternative. Our plan was to combine our office and training centre into the one location in this city. We'd been searching for more than a month without success. So yes, we had some time pressure.

The landlord, on the other hand, probably had no deadline. We had looked at the space on our own and hadn't spoken to anyone yet. While inspecting, we saw from some boxes of papers left on the floor, presumably by the previous tenant, which told us that the space had been vacant for more than 12 months. He was probably in no screaming hurry.

✓ Consider the possible opening positions

- ➤ What is the best strategy for your opening position?
- ➤ What demands or requests will you put forward?
- ➤ What will your rationale for each request be?
- ➤ What is the likely opening position of the other party?
- ➤ What demands or requests are they likely to put forward?
- ➤ What will be their rationale for each?
- ➤ Are these rationales valid or not?
- ➤ What responses could you use to counter or weaken these rationales?

I decided that our opening position would be that we were in no particular hurry. We had plenty of options — which I'm sure we did — I'd decided to put forward the criteria I have previously mentioned in my MUST HAVEs, INTEND TO HAVEs, and would be NICE TO HAVEs.

On considering what the landlord's opening position might be, I figured that he'd probably want it all — and why not!

✓ Concessions

Now it's time to consider the concessions:

➤ What concessions could you make if you had to?

➤ What would the real cost be of any such concessions? (Sometimes concessions can cost us very little, yet their value to the other party can be quite high.)

➤ Is it likely that the other party might ask for these concessions?

➤ What would be our rationale for giving these concessions?

In my rental negotiation, frankly I could accept less parking spots. Street parking wasn't bad and there were a couple of vacant lots nearby which I noticed people using for parking at no cost. Making this concession wouldn't really cost me anything.

The partitioning was also something I could concede. I didn't really expect a landlord to go along with this. We would most likely need tailor-designed partitioning wherever we went. Indeed, in some alternative sites which we had looked at, there would have been a cost for removing the existing partitioning before our partitioning could be installed.

With respect to our rationale, if we did make these concessions, we decided to make them with considerable *overtly demonstrated reluctance.* In other words, with a great deal of wailing and wringing of hands.

As we will discover later, concessions should *not* be given lightly or too quickly, if their perceived value is to be high. And concessions should not be given without asking for something in return either. We'll look at this process in considerable detail, during the Bartering Phase.

Now it's also time to look at:

➤ What concessions are you *not* prepared to make?

➤ What will your rationale be for *not* being prepared to make these concessions? (Again, later on we'll look at why having a sound reason or rationale for not giving a concession is so vitally important.)

➤ Are there some demands or requests which you should build into your opening position, for the express purpose of being able to offer them later as concessions. (The 10 car spaces and partitioning fell into this category. They were concessions built in for the express purpose of trading, if we needed to.)

✓ Conduct some market research on the other party

Consider where you can get information about them prior to your meeting?

➤ Who can you ask? — Are there newspapers, magazines, brochures, company reports, associations or industrial groups which can provide information? How about the Companies Registration Office? Are there other investigative methods that you could use?

➤ Are there ways that you might be able to find out what the other party wants or needs, in advance?

We had discovered that this landlord owned a chain of retail outlets for his importing business and with our connections in the retail scene in that city, it wasn't hard finding someone who knew the man we'd be dealing with.

As it turned out we had a mutual friend. Without telling this friend too much, I started asking questions about the man I'd soon be negotiating with. I discovered that he was a fair man, but a really keen businessman, a keen negotiator. Indeed, he'd built his business largely on his negotiating ability. However, Australia was deep in a recession at this time and retailing was not doing well. I discovered that before the recession, this man had taken the Head Lease on the entire building. That is, he didn't own the building, he had signed a lease when times were good and lease rates were high. Having that top floor empty was probably costing him in excess of $100,000 per year. This information put a whole new light on the negotiation.

Can you see how many of my previous assumptions were not valid? If I hadn't done this background research, I could have been considerably disadvantaged during the negotiation as I had strong time pressures. I now discovered that he had considerable time pressures as well as financial pressures too.

✓ Consider all sources of power

➤ What sources of power might you have on your side?
➤ What sources of power might the other party have?

(We'll be covering sources of power in detail in Part Three of this book.) However, in the case of my office rental negotiation, time pressure was one source of power which could be on both sides. My ability to relieve this landlord's financial pressure, by taking and occupying the space immediately, was a source of power on my side. There were many more sources of power at play here, as we'll discover later on.

✓ Question all assumptions

Have you made any assumptions? The answer most probably will be yes. Now it's time to look at your information and remind yourself of what is assumed and what is reality. It's enormously dangerous to mix up the two.

➤ Are these assumptions valid?
➤ What if your assumptions were not true?
➤ Are there ways you could you test your assumptions?
➤ What are the other party's likely assumptions?

➤ Do these empower you or could they be disempowering?

➤ What assumptions do you need to *correct* for the other party, to empower you and/or maybe build trust?

As you already know, I had been able to test and invalidate many of the assumptions I had initially made in this negotiating situation.

✓ Location

Now it's time to consider the "power" element of the physical location in which you will be negotiating. We all feel more confident in familiar surroundings, in other words, on our own turf.

If possible, negotiate on your own turf or on neutral ground. The environment plays an enormous role in creating the feelings in a negotiation.

For example, would you feel less or more resourceful if you were forced to negotiate in a cramped, stuffy, non air-conditioned hot room, with poor lighting, versus a cool comfortable room with lots of natural light?

Please be aware that the environment can be used to create pressure — or not.

In this rental case we decided to decline the offer made by the landlord to discuss this office space in his office. Instead we conducted all meetings standing on the floor of the empty office space itself. I'm sure he hated being reminded that it was empty too, but this was neutral ground, perfect for the negotiation, and preferable to being in his office, surrounded by his staff and all of his reminders of power and wealth.

✓ Decision-makers/decision-influencers

As far as possible it's important to ascertain:

➤ What is the decision-making process with the other party?

➤ Who will make the ultimate decision?

➤ Who will influence the decision?

➤ Are there any hidden partners or advisers? For example an accountant or lawyer.

My preference is to involve all of the decision-makers as early as possible in a negotiation. That way, a relationship is built with each of them right from the beginning.

Alternatively, consider how you might feel, and what the consequences might be, if suddenly, at what you perceive to be near the end of the negotiation, the person you've been dealing with, building rapport with, building a relationship with, suddenly informs you that he or she is not authorised to make the final decision; that the real decision-maker will be arriving in ten minutes to take over and approve or reject the deal you have been putting together for the last three weeks. The fate of the negotiation is in the hands of a stranger, a mystery person, whom you don't know, who doesn't really understand everything you've discussed with the other person and who could easily throw a spanner into the works.

Sometimes this will be a deliberate strategy called, *deferring to a higher authority* and we'll be looking at this later on.

In my rental case, we ascertained by asking him directly, that although his wife was a director of his company, he and he alone, made all decisions concerning real estate.

✓ What might the other party's negotiating style be?

➤ Will they play win/win or win/lose?

➤ Are they likely to be friendly or hostile?

➤ Will they want to move fast or slowly?

Again, there are many ways of gaining an insight into the possibilities here. Perhaps you could seek out people who have previously negotiated with this person? Or anticipate the other party's possible style?

Some negotiators like to play hard ball. That is, they take an adversarial position, a hard line approach right from the beginning. Some people like to yell and scream and get very emotional. What if you weren't expecting this? Could it throw you or cause you to feel intimidated?

By anticipating the other party's possible style, you could for example, choose a location which could render this style ineffective or cause this person to modify his or her style.

For example, I have on occasion, chosen to meet across a table in a crowded restaurant to negotiate with certain people who have a reputation for being aggressive, loud, intimidating and highly emotional in stressful circumstances. Their whole demeanour had to change in this environment, where behaviour patterns which they would normally have used, were not acceptable.

✓ How might the other party react in this negotiation?

If the negotiation is complex you may even consider acting out possible scenarios with a friend or perhaps other members of your negotiating team in preparation for the real thing. Ask someone to play the role of the other party and explore possible responses to, say, your opening position. Rehearse how you intend to handle requests which may arise. Then reverse the roles. Put yourself into the role of the person you'll be negotiating with.

Role-playing can be an invaluable exercise. It would be impossible to consider all potential variations but it can provide some useful insights and give you practice in handling some of the most likely scenarios. Then you'll feel prepared and more comfortable when it is time for the actual negotiation.

✓ How will you play in this negotiation?

➤ Will you play competitively or co-operatively?
➤ Will you take a hard line approach at the beginning and then become more co-operative?

You may care to modify your usual style to suit a particular situation or style of another person.

If he starts by playing hard ball, perhaps you may decide to match — or what is known in NLP terms, as *pace* him — in his style. Once you've matched, or paced, him you may then choose to lead him into a more co-operative style by modifying your style.

✓ What are the long/short term advantages or disadvantages of your strategies?

I negotiated recently with the management of a conference centre with which we had done business for years. On a special one-off seminar evening, where we had a particularly large audience, their charges for refreshments were way out of line with what we had been paying for our regular evenings. They argued that this evening did not fit into our existing agreement. In my opinion, they had charged excessively and I told them how I felt. However, they claimed to be within their rights and the charge stuck!

Now, the amount that was in dispute was not large — only a couple of hundred dollars. The management of the conference centre felt that it had won this negotiation. However, in the long run they had lost some $30,000 worth of our business per year, because of the ill feeling created by their short-term strategy.

✓ Are there any legal implications to consider?

I don't like to involve lawyers in negotiations but I always seek a legal opinion when I am uncertain and I've discovered that it pays to do this.

My advice is to have a lawyer who speaks plain English, and who can communicate with you in a style that you can understand. Such a lawyer can be hard to find and will always err on the side of caution when it comes to drawing up agreements. It's his job to take into consideration every possible negative outcome and contingency.

If I was to follow the cautious advice of my lawyer to the degree of detail that he makes me aware of, I don't think I'd ever sign an agreement. So in the end, I seek advice and then take full responsibility myself.

If you want to check out what I mean, take any standard loan agreement from any bank, and have your lawyer give you an opinion. It's likely he or she will point out six or more clauses which it is not in your interest to have in the agreement, yet they are used every day by thousands of people.

✓ Are there any past precedents or standard (accepted) practices to be considered in your negotiation?

Sometimes precedents can be used as a rationale for some of your demands or for countering the other party's demands.

✓ Am I the best person to negotiate in this situation?

In some situations, you may *not* be the best person to actually do the negotiating, particularly if it's a negotiation in which you are emotionally involved.

Remember, top negotiators see negotiating as simply a game. Once you become emotionally involved and it becomes serious business, you may start to give away a great deal of your power and begin to make errors in judgement.

For example, a few years ago Wendy was selling an apartment. It had gone to auction and had not reached the reserve price that she had set. The real estate agent kept bringing her offers that were still well below what she wanted. He kept telling her that she was being unrealistic in her expectations: the property simply was not worth what she was asking for it, and she should accept one of these low offers. On two occasions he came to her with a signed contract at prices $10,000 to $15,000 lower than she wanted, and deposit cheques too — very tempting!

I kept telling Wendy not to accept less than what she had in mind and reminded her that there was no real hurry to sell. However, as time dragged on, the real estate agent kept pointing out to Wendy that she had already incurred more than $4,000 in marketing and auction costs which she would have to pay, whether the property sold or not. She felt pressured, impatient and, frankly, sick and tired of the whole situation. This was exacerbated by some difficulties she was having with the tenant. She just wanted it all to be over. To say that she was emotionally involved is an understatement.

(By the way, Wendy is an excellent negotiator. However, because of her emotional involvement in this one, she was no longer the best person to be doing the negotiating.)

This was when she handed it over to me. I immediately contacted the real estate agent and told him he was no longer to speak with Wendy. I was now handling it all. As I mentioned earlier, this late introduction of a mystery man can make it very difficult for the other party. He continued to try to speak with Wendy. I continued to return all of his calls. I wasn't emotionally involved. I wasn't under any pressure. I told him that I didn't think he had any really serious buyers and that I would find a buyer myself. Within a week he came back with an offer $5,000 higher. I told him to forget it, that I was just about to conclude negotiations with a serious buyer who was offering what Wendy now wanted. Within 24 hours I had a signed contract with a deposit from this real estate agent for a price acceptable to us and the sale went through.

Being emotionally involved could have cost Wendy more than $10,000. Recognising this was a smart move on her part.

So consider this question: "Is there someone else who should be fronting for you, who would be less emotionally involved or who might produce a better outcome for you?

As you can see, there are a great many issues to be considered during the Preparation Phase of a negotiation. Whether you take all of these areas into account will depend on the negotiation. However, recognise that the average person does very little preparation, while a master negotiator does his or her homework first, and it makes a major difference.

Let's look now at the second phase of our negotiating model, the subject of rapport.

Counter Instinctive Negotiating Phase # 2

RAPPORT

Over the last 20 years or so, I have read innumerable books, and have been to many, many training programmes, which at some stage dealt with this subject of rapport. We're told that rapport is important. To be "in rapport" with a person is necessary if we want to sell to them. But very few of these books or courses have ever told me why or how to "do rapport" or even what "rapport" really is.

I asked a seminar group recently, "What is rapport?"

Some of their answers really surprised me.

"It's getting someone to like you!" said some people. "It's getting on with someone," said others. So what is rapport, really?

One dictionary definition of rapport is "a harmonious understanding relationship".

Well maybe there's a clue there. Rapport certainly has something to do with building a relationship. But a "harmonious relationship", what does that mean and how does one do that?

Again, if we look to the dictionary for a clue, "harmonious" is defined as: "forming a pleasing whole; free from disagreement".

Now, that could be useful in a negotiation but how do we do that?

I found the answer through my study of Neuro Linguistic Programming (NLP). My friend and NLP mentor, Roger Deaner, explains that rapport — in NLP terms — is defined like this: "When we seek to reduce the differences between ourselves and another person, at a non-verbal as well as verbal level, at a level below the conscious awareness of the other person."

By the way, it's not necessarily making the other person like you. Roger says that building rapport is: "Where you minimise the difference and maximise the 'sameness' between you and the other person."

So in the context of this book, when I speak of rapport, this is what I'm referring to.

If, for example, the other person was displaying behaviour which showed a *dislike* of you, and you were using behaviour which was trying to make this person *like* you then, in fact, you would be *increasing*, not *decreasing* the difference between the two of you. Have you ever experienced that?

Can you recall a situation where you, or maybe someone you knew, wanted to remain distant, cool and unresponsive to another person, while that other person was gushing and being overly attentive? How did that make you or this person feel? Frankly, it can drive you crazy, can't it? It can drive a wedge even deeper between the two of you.

So, if someone chooses to use the behaviour of say, mild conflict, we may need to respond the same way, to actually be in rapport. How useful will that be in a negotiation, if we are both using, say, conflict-type behaviour?

The answer is very useful, as we'll discover later. At least we would now be in rapport, and once we are in rapport we may choose to use our rapport-building skills to then "lead" the other person, to modify their behaviour to a more resourceful and more useful state.

You may have already come across some of the terminology for this process. It's sometimes called, *pacing, matching* or *mirroring*. The part you may be less familiar with, is called *leading*.

Can we really lead another individual to use behaviour which is more useful to our negotiation? Stay tuned, and you'll find out how. Understand though, that it all starts with being in rapport, which is why knowing how to "do rapport" is so important.

How can we begin to build rapport with another person?

It begins by having respect for the way in which the other person processes the world. Of course, this could be vastly different to how we process the world. In other words, the way I see the world may not be the same way that you see the world. So does that make me right and you wrong?

Of course not! We just have a different perspective of the same situation.

Similarly, my outward behaviour, will probably be a reflection of my inner world or how I see the world, and yes, that behaviour may be different to your behaviour. Again, this doesn't make my behaviour right and your behaviour wrong — just different.

So building rapport — reducing the differences, and increasing the sameness — probably begins with being prepared to examine the world from the other person's perspective. So how can we do this?

Pacing

This is where pacing comes in. Pacing is the process by which you can establish and maintain rapport, by moving as the other person moves.

So any behaviour that you can identify, you can pace. You do this by adjusting your own behaviour, both verbal and non-verbal, to move with the other person at both a physical and a psychological level.

However, there is an important rule to bear in mind here. Roger says we must be "graceful" and "respectful" in our pacing, so that the other person is not aware of what we are doing at a conscious level. Rather, they will become aware of this sameness only at an unconscious level and may simply begin to feel more comfortable with us — sense that we are more like them than perhaps they initially thought.

So physically, what can we do to build this rapport through pacing?

You already know the answer to this! You do this all the time at an unconscious level with people you get along with. What I'd like to do now is simply make you consciously aware of what it is that you do when you get along with someone. If you knew specifically what it was that you were already doing, you could do it on purpose.

We call this moving from being *unconsciously competent* to being *consciously competent*. By the way, this is vital if we are to become consciously counter intuitive in our negotiating because right now we may be instinctively choosing behaviour which does *not* build rapport but seeks to satisfy our own inner needs. For example, many people have an instinctive need to be liked, rather than be in conflict.

If you have any doubt about what I'm about to say, begin to study people who are in obvious rapport, in say social or business situations, and look at what they are doing, unconsciously.

Let's get started with a list of methods of pacing. Remember "graceful and respectful" — be subtle.

Body language

The first area we're going to look at to pace is the other person's body language.

(This is certainly not a new subject. Allan Pease wrote a best-selling book on this more than a decade ago, and has built a very successful career on it.)

To pace somebody physically we can:

➤ **Match their entire — or even part of — their body positioning**. So if they are slouching, we can "gracefully and respectfully" slowly begin to move our body to very much the same position as theirs. As they move and change, we can move and change too, just after they do. If they lean back and place their hands behind their head, so do we. If they stand up, then so do we. As I said, you are already doing this sort of thing every day with people you get along with.

➤ **Match their head and shoulders angle**. Notice how some people tilt their head and hold their shoulders at an angle to you. Maybe you've never noticed this before. Begin to notice now and to match them.

➤ **Match their facial expressions**. People sometimes squint as they make a point, or they move their forehead as they speak. Start to match this.

➤ **Match their gestures**. Some people wave their hands around as they speak and point, don't they? Begin to notice the gestures people use and practice matching or pacing these gestures.

The voice

The second part of pacing deals with voice qualities. What I mean is tonality, tempo of speech, volume and intensity.

Let's face it, if someone is speaking quietly and we are in rapport, we speak quietly too, don't we? What if we don't? Well, it could be seen by the other person as impolite or inappropriate, and they'll start to feel uncomfortable. They probably won't even be able to pinpoint why. They'll just get a feeling. Try it and see for yourself some time.

Haven't you seen this happen, with maybe someone who has had too much to drink? They speak loudly and rather than building rapport, they are destroying it.

Experiment with tonality, matching the other person's tone of voice too. Try matching the tempo of their speech. If they speak fast, you speak fast too.

Phraseology

You may have noticed how some people use certain phrases on a repetitive basis. They'll say things like: "and would you believe....", and: "ya know what I mean", and: "my goodness"!

Look out for such phrases, and if they use them repetitively, begin to use them yourself.

Representational Systems

Now this is a big subject all on its own, and I'm not going to go into extraordinary detail here, because it's a part of a much bigger NLP discipline. You may care to do some courses or listen to some tapes on this powerful technology. In 1993, I began the journey of exploration into NLP, with a five-month long NLP Practitioner programme — and I'm still learning every day.

So what do I mean by representational systems in verbal language?

Well, one of the issues that NLP deals with, is how we represent our world in language — that is, linguistically — when we talk to ourselves and others.

Here are five channels, or representational systems, that we all use (and by the way, we tend to favour certain channels over others, at certain times, as we communicate).

These five channels are:

➤ Visual channel — how we see things

➤ Auditory channel — what we hear

➤ Kinesthetic channel — what we touch physically or feel "inside"

➤ Gustatory channel — what we taste

➤ Olfactory channel — what we smell.

The three primary channels we tend to use most frequently are visual, auditory and kinesthetic.

So when a person is favouring their visual channel and using a **visual representational** system when they are communicating, they will use words and phrases which are very visual. For example they'll say: "I *see* what you mean." "*Looks* good to me." "I just lit up when I could *see* the bright *picture* of the future he was painting for me." And they will use lots of visual predicates and words.

A person favouring their **auditory representational** system may say: "I *hear* what you're saying". "*Sounds* good to me". " It was like *music to my ears* when I *heard* the sound plans he had for the future". Notice the many auditory predicates.

A person favouring their **kinesthetic representational** system would say something like: "I've got a fair *grasp* on what you're saying." "*Feels* good to me", " I *felt* a wave of excitement come over me as it got through to me, the vibrant future that I could *feel* coming my way".

The words that people use in their conversation are not chosen at random. Rather they are chosen to represent the world as they are experiencing it at that time. People are not "Visuals", "Auditories" or "Kinesthetics" as such. Their representational systems may change from circumstance to circumstance. However, the words they use on the outside are indicative of the words they are using to talk to themselves on the inside.

If we match these visual, auditory or kinesthetic words, we will literally be on their more favoured wave-length for communication at that time. We've all heard the phrase: "we just weren't on the same wave-length", from people who were not getting along together, and they were probably right. At an unconscious level they probably were on different wave-lengths, with different representational systems, which was a part of why they were not feeling in rapport with each other.

You see, we tend to favour particular representational systems at different times, when we speak. Matching the other person's representational system will build rapport and this very definitely happens at an unconscious level. They won't even notice any shift in phraseology. They'll just notice at an unconscious level, that we are "like them" somehow.

Breathing

The third way in which you can pace another person deals with breathing. Yes, breathing! This is very subtle.

Notice how the other person is breathing. Are they breathing deeply or with quick shallow breaths. For example, if people are nervous they will tend to breath quickly and their breathing may be shallow.

Matching their breathing is fairly easy. Just watch the rise and fall of their shoulders or chest for the clues you need.

Again this rapport is very much at an unconscious level.

General Behaviour

This is the fourth part of pacing. For example, what if you notice that the other person favours communicating in writing or by fax? What if you notice that they like to dress casually whereas you may prefer to dress more formally for your meetings?

You may choose to pace them by matching this behaviour and again for some reason they'll just begin to feel that you are in many ways just the same as them.

So there is quite a deal to know about building rapport, isn't there? Is it easy to "track" for — or notice — all of these things about the other person and then to match them?

Initially you may find it challenging. So my suggestion is to simply take on one chunk at a time and begin to notice these things more about the people you interact with every day. As time goes on you'll find it more and more easy to match — and thus to pace — people and the result will be greater rapport with more and more people, and that can be useful in all areas of life, can't it?

Incidentally, the more you begin to physically match another person's physiology, the more you'll be able to match their psychological interpretation of the world. In other words, the more you match the other person, the more you'll begin to understand *how* they are thinking, and *how* they see the negotiating situation. This can be very helpful, wouldn't you agree?

By the way, rapport is an on-going process, not just a step in the negotiation. You don't just "do rapport" and then move to the next step. Maintaining rapport throughout the entire negotiation is important.

Breaking Rapport

Now that you have a better understanding of how to build rapport, you will also have a better understanding of how to break it. That is, how to make the other person feel *uncomfortable* with you. Again, you can do this at a level below the other person's conscious awareness.

So why would you want to break rapport?

Let's say for example that the other party suddenly resorted to some behaviour which you didn't want them to use. Let's say they suddenly moved to being loud and aggressive, from being quiet and co-operative.

You can, at an unconscious level, begin to reward the behaviour you want to elicit and punish the behaviour you find undesirable. You do this by being *in rapport* when they demonstrate the desired behaviour, and by *breaking rapport* when they use behaviour that you don't like.

Could this be possible? Could this really work to influence another person at an unconscious level, to use the behaviour that you want? You bet! This is very powerful technology, and really only the tip of the NLP iceberg. That's why I suggest that you may care to look into NLP in more depth.

Certainly, I'll be talking more about NLP, and its application to negotiating, right throughout this book. If you are already an expert in NLP, you may find my explanations very simplistic. That's OK, I like to keep things simple, don't you?

Leading

I spoke earlier about the term "leading". I suggested that once you were in rapport with another person, you may then care to lead them to other behaviour which you consider more appropriate for producing the outcome you desire in the negotiation.

So what do I mean by "lead" and how can you do this?

Well, it all starts with being in rapport with the other person. So if you would seek to modify another's behaviour, you must first minimise the differences between you, using all of the rapport-building skills we've been discussing here.

When you are in rapport you can begin to use those same skills to lead the person to change their physiology and to follow you.

For example, if you are in rapport, and the person you're talking with is leaning back — which may indicate remoteness — you first match them and then after some time you lean forward, they may then follow you into this more co-operative position.

If the person is stressed and nervous and perhaps you want them to be more relaxed, you may care to slow down *your* rate of speech, lower the tone of *your* voice, begin to breath more deeply and more slowly, relaxing *your* body more and so on, a little at a time. You may find the other person following you into this more resourceful state.

Again, the words "gracefully and respectfully" are important.

So, there we have it. There is a lot more to rapport than most people understand. Develop rapport-building skills and you have a great tool that can be used in so many situations.

Let's look now at the next phase of our negotiating model.

Counter Instinctive Negotiating Phase # 3
GATHERING INFORMATION

This is where we begin to get down to business; where we seek to discover what the other party really wants as an outcome to this negotiation.

From our preparation we may have a fair idea of what the other party wants, but now it's time to test our assumptions, to see whether some of the assumptions we have made are perhaps inaccurate, which of course they could be.

This is the phase where we will seek to have the other party state their opening position, (and please understand that it is precisely that, their *opening* position).

They may say they want all manner of things at this stage, but in reality, there could be a vast difference between what they say they want and what, they will in the end be prepared to settle for. So please keep this in mind as you begin to elicit their opening position.

During this phase of gathering information you will be seeking to ascertain their HAP, which as you will recall stands for their Highest Advanced Position, their ideal best scenario for an outcome.

You'll be seeking to understand their:

➤ MUST HAVEs, INTEND TO HAVEs, NICE TO HAVEs.

➤ Real intentions behind their requests; some indication of their timeframe, possible deadlines and other pressures.

➤ Financial budget, or the dollars that the other party may think are involved.

➤ Who the ultimate decision-maker will be, as well as who might influence any such decisions

➤ How the other party may intend to play in this negotiation — win/win, win/lose, co-operative or competitive, hard ball and so on.

You'll also be putting forward your opening position. So that raises the question, who should put forward their position first? Who should say what they are looking for first?

Well as a general rule, I like to "frame up" the negotiation first, putting forward my views on how I'd like to see the negotiating process happen and then invite the other party to "share" with me their views on where they are coming from, how they see the situation now, and how they'd like to see "us" work it all out together.

The only exception to this let-them-go-first rule is where I am fairly certain that their request or desired outcome is going to be greatly mismatched to mine.

For example, let's say I'm buying something and I've decided that I'm only willing to go as far as say $38,000, (which incidentally, is not the amount I'll mention first). Yet, from my research I know that the other person has a vastly different perception of the value of the item. Let's say I'm sure that they are looking for at least $60,000 for it. This is where I will want to put forward my views first, complete with my justifications on the value of the item, before they put forward their views. In introducing my views first, I may considerably lower the other party's expectations right off, before we even get started.

By the way, be aware that this tactic may also be used *against* you when the other party puts forward their view first. Don't let this influence you or cause you to reassess your opening position, or lower your expectations.

In most cases, then, it's desirable to let the other party get everything off their chest first. This allows you to access the situation before you open your mouth. If this negotiation involves a stressful or emotional issue, by allowing the other party to go first while you listen quietly and attentively, you may cause them to feel more relaxed, less aggressive and, in some situations, I've even seen remorse set in immediately after I've been on the receiving end of a barrage of verbal abuse, at the opening of the negotiation.

The Law of Psychological Reciprocity

The law of psychological reciprocity often kicks in at this point, too, in most situations. This law says: "when you extend a courtesy or kindness to another person, under most circumstances, that person will then feel psychologically obliged, to extend the same, or a similar consideration to you."

So if you sit quietly and attentively, and listen with courtesy, this sets the tone for how the other party may, in turn, listen and respond to you.

Let's go back to something I mentioned before. I said I like to "frame up" or set the "frame", right at the beginning, for how I would like to see the negotiating process go.

Let's face it, sometimes at the outset of a negotiation we may not be able to find a great deal to agree upon. So always try to set what I call an agree-to-agree frame.

That is, I begin by trying to find some common ground; something that we both would like to find out. It might be how we could work things out together for the benefit and best interests of both parties. If we can agree to agree on that then we're off to a great start.

I then see if we can agree-to-agree on the way we might go about this, and in this manner I seek to gain some agreement on our "rules for the game". In other words, I put forward how I'd like to play the game. I suggest a co-operative approach where we work together to create win/win.

For example, I see if we can agree to agree that:

➤ We will both seek to understand the other person's view point or at least to listen

➤ We will both try to remain calm and courteous

➤ We will concentrate only on certain issues on this occasion. This can be very important to prevent becoming diverted from the main issues and be distracted by side issues of much lesser importance. Sometimes it's also necessary to broaden the scope of issues. If discussions focus on just one issue, such as price, and we can't agree on the price, then there must be a winner and a loser, and that's not going to create win/win or good feeling. There are many more facets to a negotiation than just the dollars.

➤ We will concentrate on these issues rather than the personalities involved, and try not to get personal.

➤ We will play win/win, where we will seek to have both parties come out feeling that they have won.

If this is not a one-shot deal, if we will be interacting again in the future, I try to gain some agreement that we must create an outcome on this occasion, which will allow for a successful on-going relationship. In other words, the outcome of the negotiation this time should not cause irreparable damage to this on-going relationship.

Then it's time to find out what this other party wants. We might start with questions such as:

➤ So where are *you* coming from?

➤ How do *you* see the situation?

➤ How do *you* see that this has come about?

➤ Ideally, what would *you* like to come out of our discussions?

➤ Why do *you* want that?

➤ How do *you* mean?

➤ Why is that important to *you?*

➤ What would that mean to *you?*

This is where we seek to understand the other party's intention behind any requests that they may have. It's important that the other party be as specific as possible, too, on what they want and tell you *why* they want these things.

Listen carefully at this stage in negotiations and even take notes. What is really going on for the other person, *behind* what they are saying? Often, it's what is *not* said that is important. Try to draw the other person out to discuss their *feelings* about the issue, not just the issues themselves.

Also, encourage the other person to prioritise their wants and needs. Quiz them on the justification or rationalisation for their requests. Perhaps ask: "Why do you feel that would be fair?"

Make sure *all* of their wants and needs are revealed *before* you begin to reveal your own. Check and double check that you have everything — "Is there anything else? Are you sure?". And even then don't assume that you have them all.

(By the way, now is not the time to start bartering or trading concessions. All we want right here is to get all of the issues on the table.)

In the next stage of the negotiation, after you've gathered this information, you'll be putting forward your requests and probing and exploring the options available.

Counter Instinctive Negotiating Phase # 4
PROBING AND EXPLORING OPTIONS

This is where we explore the options available and sometimes discover how flexible or inflexible the other party is. We may even be able to establish the possible range of the negotiation — how high and how low they may or may not be prepared to go.

There are two ways you can approach this phase. You can frame this as a *competitive* process or you can frame this as a *co-operative* process, where you are working together to come up with possible options to satisfy the needs of both parties. In other words to create win/win.

My suggestion in most cases is to frame it as a co-operative process. Remember, it is easy to move from co-operative to competitive if you need to later on. It is almost impossible to move from hard-line competitive to co-operative.

Let me illustrate: "I think you are a complete moron! There is no way, I would do business with you except totally on my terms. You're a liar, a cheat, your family stinks, you're an idiot, I would never trust you, and I don't like you either."

Now that's what I call a competitive, hard-line opening position, and because of the law of psychological reciprocity, we are likely to receive a similar opening position back. The negotiation may reach a stalemate right at the beginning. This helps nobody. So what are you going to do now? You can't very well say: "Hey, maybe I came on a bit strong there a minute ago, I hope you weren't offended. And that crack about your family... well maybe I was a little out of line."

Are you kidding? The damage has been done. It's hard to reverse. So what if the other party opens this way?

The skilled negotiator will not respond in a like manner. Remember what we said about counter instinctive responses? Instead, Top Gun negotiators will stick to their original game plan to broaden the issues and to discuss options.

We are not yet ready to start trading concessions either, we'll do that in the Bartering Phase. Right now, all we simply wish to do is explore some of the options.

We are not putting forward offers here, we are simply talking in terms of theory, and it's important that the other party understands this.

So let's consider how we might frame this stage with the other party. We may open by saying: "Before we really get down to business here, could we just talk about some of the options available to both of us? "May I first ask, ideally, what would you like to see as the outcome of our discussions here today?

And when they respond, you may care to use a technique which we'll be talking a lot more about later. It's called the *flinch.*

No matter what they say you flinch — "What? You want what?" or "You're joking, right?"

The flinch is a very valuable technique to remember to use. Its purpose is to lower the other party's expectations. By the way, watch what happens when you use the flinch, even when in your own mind you like what they are suggesting. Maybe it's even better than you had expected, still flinch.

Why?

Well, as I said, firstly it lowers the other party's expectations. They may adjust their thinking downwards in terms of their demands before the real negotiations even start. Secondly, if you later agree to this request, they will then place a greater value on gaining this item. It will be perceived as a concession that you are making for them. So if you make a concession you'll be asking for a concession from them in return. The third reason for the flinch is that people generally place more value on what they have to work hard for, than on things that come easy!

So let's get back to their response to your original question: "What would you like to see as the outcome of our discussions here today?"

No matter what the response is, question it. Seek clarification. Try to understand what they really mean. You may start with: "So why would that be important to you?"

(By the way, we may have to ask this question several times, to peel away the layers, to reveal the real intention behind what they are saying.)

Remember that dumb is smart in negotiating! Your next major question might be: "In the longer term, what would you like to see happen?"

Wait for a response, and then question it: "So why would that really be important to you?", "Why is that?", "How do you mean?" And then you might ask, if it's appropriate: "What would you like our relationship to be?", "So why would that be important to you?", "Why is that?", "How do you mean?"

You're testing their flexibility now, and by the way, remember that rapport and personal resourcefulness are important here. You will not get far with this questioning unless you have established rapport and unless you do feel resourceful, empowered and confident.

Again, you may care to use the flinch — "You want what?" — before you again question their responses.

Then ask the questions again: "What if that were not possible? What would the next best outcome be as you see it? What would we then have to do?"

You may care to use the flinch here too, before you question their responses: "So why would that be important to you?", "Why is that?", "How do you mean?"

After you have discovered just how flexible or inflexible the other party is, and what the options are as they perceive the situation, then it's time to float a few of the options that you see as being viable.

(By the way, because of the information you now have, you will be in a much better position, too, to judge what their responses will be to the options that you put forward. You are less likely to have surprise responses that could throw an unskilled negotiator off track.)

Remember at this time, you are *not* putting forward any concrete offers, you are still just talking in theory! — "Well, I'm just talking in theory here now, but supposing for a moment that I was looking for..." And state your ideal scenarios here: "How would you feel about this?

After you ask this question, it's important to be absolutely quiet and to listen. Don't be afraid of silence. It is a very powerful tool in a negotiation. Use it. Wait for a response, no matter how long it takes. Examine your pen while you wait for an answer. Do anything you like, but don't be tempted to jump in and help them with their answer.

Remember also, right now it's just theory and all you are doing is floating options and looking for a response. You may be surprised at the responses that you get too.

Watch out for a flinch here from them too. A skilled negotiator will flinch. It's intended to lower your expectations, but don't respond to a flinch. If you do, they'll continue to use it.

Sometimes you'll find that their response to something that you thought would outrage them, is very positive. Alternatively, you may find that something, which you thought would be no problem at all, evokes a negative or even hostile reaction. Be ready for this.

Whatever their response is, remain calm and remember that this process is only a game and we are just talking theory right now. If their response is hostile, remind them of this.

Understand also that these options that you are floating now, will affect the expectations of the other party. Aim high. Go for *beyond* what you really want and look at the response you are getting, or not getting. You may be very surprised.

In a real estate deal that I was involved in recently, I knew that the other party was looking for half a million dollars for the property. I thought, just for fun, I'd float the option of $397,500. As I did this, I expected them to be totally outraged, so I started by explaining that I really would like to be able to pay what they were asking for — it was a beautiful piece of property — but I could only offer $397,500 because that's all the cash I had available. Could they possibly help me? Could we possibly work something out?

I sat back and waited for what I thought would be either outrage or laughter. We sat in silence for what seemed an eternity. Then the real estate agent, who was acting on behalf of a client I hadn't been able to meet yet, turned to his associate in the office, rubbed his chin (so did I — remember rapport!), they both shook their heads, and responded with: "Well, I suppose we could discuss this with them."

What had I discovered? I had discovered that they were far more flexible on the price than my market research had previously revealed. I repressed my surprise, remembering that counter instinctive responses are the best responses, while inside I was going, "Yippee, Yahooo!!! I can't believe this!"

(By the way, it's important to support any of these options that you float with sound reasons for this possible expectation on your part, and be ready to expand on your logical reasoning.)

I reasoned that I'd been studying the real estate market in that area for two months and that based on the outcomes of numerous auctions I'd attended, this was what this property was probably really worth. I gave some specific examples of properties that I thought they probably knew, and gave the exact figures that they'd settled for. I could see that they knew I was indeed well informed.

Now, whatever their response is, be it positive or negative, remember to question it, looking again for the real intention behind their words: "So why do you feel that way?", "Why is that?", "How do you mean?"

This is particularly important if their response is negative, or they have an objection to the option you have just floated.

Smoking out the Real Objection

In our TOP GUN® Sales Course we teach a technique for what we call, "smoking out the real objection". You see, people don't always say what's really on their mind. Very often they will give you a reason which is not really why they are objecting.

The unskilled negotiator will then either waste time trying to handle a reason or an objection which doesn't actually exist, or will accept their objection and drop their request.

Let me share this technique with you right now. You will find it illustrated opposite. We call it The Stair Step Method For Handling Objections.

By the way, if you use this technique every time, just knowing that you now have a planned response to every objection, will empower you, calm you and boost your confidence.

Increased confidence will come from practising this technique, and the more practice you get, the more natural this will sound.

Here's our response to a negative objection:

Step 1

"Obviously you must have a reason for saying that John, do you mind if I ask what it is?"

John says no, he doesn't mind. So you ask: "What is it?"

Let's say John simply says, "I could never go along with what you've just suggested!" And when you ask:

"Obviously you must have a reason for saying that, John, do you mind if I ask what it is?"

He says: "Well you're asking too much money for that. I simply can't afford that!"

The Stair Step Method For Handling Objections

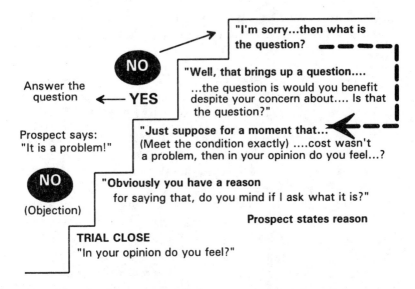

Step 2

Your next step is to satisfy the condition John has just stated — meet it exactly — and then listen for the response. You do that by saying:

"Just supposing for a moment that wasn't a problem, that money wasn't an issue, then in your opinion do you feel this option would be possible?"

John will say either "Yes!" or "No!" Let's say he says "No!" again. What have we discovered now? It's not just John's lack of money. There is another issue, a hidden issue, that we need to bring out. So we ask that original question again, adding one word.

"John, obviously you must have some *other* reason for saying that, do you mind if I ask what that is?"

Now John may something like, "Well, even if I could get that much money together, I couldn't come up with it right away." So what have we found out now? It may be that John is really not objecting to the price, perhaps the problem is really with the terms. If the terms were different, could John come up with the asking price after all?

Step 3

"John, just supposing that you didn't have to come up with all of the cash right away, then in your opinion do you feel that this option has some possibilities?"

What have we done? Again, we've met his condition exactly to test its validity. John may now say: "Well, yes, it could work, but I really would need some terms to come up with that sort of cash."

What have we discovered? We've discovered that the amount of money was not the main problem. There was another problem — terms — and another possible option which could be now floated, concerning terms.

This technique of questioning all negatives or objections, moves you beyond a possible obstacle or impasse. Remember, we are still only talking options here.

As you explore these objections, make a note, in writing, of what possible options you are being offered by the other party, and record their justifications or rationalisations for each of these. Later you may want to counter these rationalisations.

Also note down what options and scenarios are being put forward by you, which have been accepted by them. You may need to show them these notes later, so keep good records. People in our culture have a strong need to remain consistent with what they've previously suggested or agreed to. So you may need to remind them of these things.

It may now be necessary to take time out to consider all of these options before you move to the next phase of this model of negotiating — the Bartering Phase.

Don't be afraid to *ask* for time out either. Slow the negotiation process down. The more time a person invests in a negotiation, the more emotional attachment he will have to the outcome, and very often, the more flexible the other party becomes. We'll talk more about this later.

Counter Instinctive Negotiating Phase # 5
BARTERING

In the Probing Phase we invited the other party to put forward *their* requests and now it's time to confirm what *we* are looking for. This is also the phase where we start exchanging concessions. By the way, concessions can be very positive, without them there would be no negotiating.

We also spoke earlier about "building in" certain requests for the specific purpose of trading them as concessions later on. So by now the other party will have either specifically requested that we make certain concessions, or by understanding what they want, we can see that they may be looking for some.

I like to think of the Bartering Phase as a process of giving and taking.

Making Demands

Let's talk about how to construct a winning demand. By the way, I'd never call it a demand in a win/win negotiating situation. It's a *request to satisfy a need*.

Now, the major point that I'd like to make about verbalising our requests or our "demands" is that for every demand we make, we should have a well thought out rationale, or reason for this demand; the stronger the rationale, the stronger the negotiating demand.

For example: "I need a minimum of ten car spaces included in this lease because I have key staff coming and going all day long with heavy equipment. They'll need to be able to park near the elevator. Street parking is out of the question for them because it would be too far to carry this equipment."

Let's talk now about the art of giving concessions, and yes, when it's done properly, it really is an art.

Giving Concessions

All concessions should have two parts, the "give" and the "take". If they don't, you will be missing a major opportunity to make gains in the negotiation. Frankly, most unskilled negotiators miss these opportunities every time — but not you.

For every concession that you make from now on, you will seek to get something in return. So each concession that you make becomes conditional — "I'll agree to make this concession for you, however, if I do I'll do so only providing you agree to....." — and we then state our demand, complete with our rationale for this demand. So in a sense, the condition becomes a counter-demand.

By the way, for every concession we *give*, we should have a well thought out rationale for the concession. It's as important to have a strong rationale for giving a concession as it is for making a demand. So let me give you a simple structure for making concessions, using a counter demand:

Concession — "OK, I will agree to accept just five car spaces..."

Rationale — "Because, I think I could persuade my people to share these spots for loading and unloading, and then put their cars on the street..."

Condition or Conditions — "Providing you (or if you) agree to a month-by-month rental rather than a 12 month lease, OK?"

So that's the structure in three parts.

> **Step 1** — State the concession you're prepared to make, but remember to make the concession reluctantly, even if it's an easy concession to make. I like to call it, "Hollywooding" the concession, making a big song and dance about it before agreeing.

> **Step 2** — Provide some rationale as to how you can now justify making this concession after all.

> **Step 3** — State the conditions which would have to be met by the other party in order for you to make this concession. In other words, your counter demand.

Make Sure You Have All The Demands

And here's a final thought, don't concede until you are sure that you have all the demands that relate to that concession out in the open.

A very common mistake made by inexperienced negotiators is to agree to make a concession only to find that they are then immediately asked to make another one.

So how do we avoid this? I call it *Bundling Demands*.

When you are being asked to make a concession in response to a demand, before you make any move, ask the question: "Before I give you my response to that, is there anything else you want?"

For example, I was buying some furniture recently and we were in the Bartering Phase. I negotiated the store owner down to his rock bottom price, then I pointed out that his competitor had agreed to throw in a lamp and some cushions. I suggested that he would probably want to do this too. His face dropped as he realised that he had not allowed for this in his margin. Reluctantly he agreed to this demand as well.

And then as he wrote up the invoice and I saw a delivery fee of $20, I said, "Well, I would have thought that delivery was included. Your competitor certainly wasn't going to charge me delivery. You will deliver it free, won't you?" What could he say?

Again, this process is called "nibbling" and one of the ways to stop it is to get all of the other party's demands out in the open, bundle them together, and then give just one concession in exchange for all of them.

On the other hand, when you are making demands, it's important to have each request handled separately, "unbundled" so to speak, just as I was doing in this case

So with concessions, we're talking in terms of trade offs. Here is the concession structure again below. Try it yourself.

> **Step 1** — State the concession you're prepared to make:...
....
....

> **Step 2** — Provide some rationale as to how you can now justify making this concession after all:........
....
....
....

> **Step 3** — State the conditions which would have to be met by the other party in order for you to make this concession...
....
....
....

Keeping Score

Let's talk for a moment now about keeping score. When either you or the other party makes a concession, it's important to write it down. If you don't, this concession may be forgotten about later on. You'll also need these notes in the Confirming Phase or, what I like to call the Nailing Down Phase of the negotiation. This is where we restate what each party has agreed to and get final agreement on the outcome of the overall negotiation.

The other reason for keeping score is to ensure that we are not being asked to make more concessions than the other party has been prepared to make.

So here's how keeping the score works.

"John, I'm sorry but I really can't move on until you make this concession. You see, I've been keeping score here and I have all of these ticks on this side of the page. This is my side, and these are all the concessions I've made for you. And this is your side, the concessions you have made for me. I really need another tick on your side of the page before we can move on. Come on now, John, play fair, OK?"

Then be quiet and wait for a response. You'll be surprised just how effective this technique can be.

The Size of Concessions

The size of the concessions that we, or the other party is prepared to make, sets up expectations — both positive and negative — in the mind of the other party.

It can also indicate where the other party is, in relation to their "bottom line". Understanding this, we can also lead the other party to believe that we have reached our bottom line, when indeed we may still have some considerable flexibility available. This can be very desirable in stopping the grinding down process which so frequently occurs in negotiations.

Giving big concessions can convey that you are very flexible, and that you may be able to go even further. By the way, if you make the mistake of giving a big concession first, and going all the way to your bottom line in one go, the other party is likely to want even more because of this perceived flexibility. If you then can't give any more, the other party may feel that you are really holding out on them, and this creates bad feeling, making them less likely to give you concessions.

Remember, people really only appreciate what they have worked hard to get and rarely appreciate what they get easily. Don't forget that negotiating is not just about the bottom line. It's a game where people's feelings count.

Giving small concessions, or if we're talking dollars giving concessions in small increments, conveys that you are not able to be very flexible, and can make the other party feel good about negotiating you down.

Let me give you an example of what I mean.

Let's say it's a real estate negotiation on a small apartment, and the asking price is $100,000.

"$100,000!!!" You gasp, (remembering the power of the flinch), and so they immediately drop to $80,000. Now $20,000, that's a pretty big concession to make on a $100,000 property — 20 per cent! What expectation does this set up in your mind?

Wouldn't you think: "Hey, they really weren't that serious about getting that $100,000. They're probably prepared to go even lower!" So you press them even harder. They move to say $75,000 — a smaller increment this time — just 6.25 per cent, and then to $74,500, just 0.6 per cent.

What expectation would you now have? "They're probably getting near their bottom line". Their concessions are getting smaller — just $500 that time. There's probably not much more to go, if anything."

You see, it's not just the concessions you make, it's how you make them.

Contrast this with how a skilled negotiator might handle this same situation.

Firstly, let's say they have set their bottom line at $90,000 to avoid ending up as the previous negotiator did at $74,000 or less. Firstly they will start higher at, say, $110,000.

You flinch and they ignore this flinch.

You ask them to make a concession, stating that your rationale for this concession is that you've noticed there is a glut of similar apartments on the market in this area right now, and that in your opinion the apartment is nice, but not really worth $110,000. You "low ball" them with an offer of just $80,000. You know that it's worth more than this, but it's always wise to start low.

Now *he* flinches. "$80,000!!! You've got to be joking. You'll have to do better than that!"

So you "to and fro" until he says: "Well I might be prepared to move a little on the price..... but if I do this for you, what can you do for me?" He's setting it up now for a conditional concession. That's smart.

Being a good negotiator yourself, you ask him about terms and suggest that you might be able to arrange a faster than 90 day settlement, if he can come down on the price.

He says: "OK, I will agree to come down to $105,000... because, if you can give me fast settlement that will save me on interest and I can pass that on to you..." (rationalisation.) "Providing you agree to a 30 day settlement. OK?" (condition and counter demand).

What expectation does that set up in your mind? He's come down by just 4.5 per cent as opposed to 20 per cent. He's not giving much away, is he? He wants something in return too. He's really making you work for this concession.

So you offer him a 60 day settlement, instead of the 30 days he wanted telling him: "You'll have to do better than that for a 30 day settlement!"

He comes back now with $103,500. That's just a 1.4 per cent reduction. His concessions are getting smaller. You barter some more.

He comes back with $102,990. That's less than 0.5 per cent. And if he's a good negotiator he'll be asking for concessions from you in exchange for these concessions. He's made you work hard for these concessions and thus made you feel that you've done well.

The Lesson

So what have we learnt here?

➤ When you make concessions, do so slowly, reluctantly and starting small, and then continue in ever-diminishing increments. This will convey that you are reaching the low end of your negotiating range and will stop the grinding away process.

➤ Always make your offer above your goal if you are selling, and below your goal if you are buying.

➤ Make the other person work hard for the concessions you give — then he'll appreciate the victory even more. In this case, he's finished $12,990 above his real bottom line.

This is precisely what happens in the real world every day. Which is why two identical apartments, owned by two different owners, will sell in the same building, in the same month, and there will be a $20,000 difference in what they have sold for. It's the skill of the negotiator that makes the difference.

Final Offer

In making your final offer, it's important to frame it as your absolute final, final offer, and again provide a strong rationalisation as to why this will be your final offer.

In making a final offer, I believe you must be prepared to walk away if it's not accepted.

Now, does this mean you can't walk back again? Of course not. There is only one thing that will stop a person re-opening negotiations and that's pride which can be an expensive indulgence.

By now if you've negotiated well up to this point, the other party has made a considerable investment in you already. They have invested their time, (which could be worth money to them), their energy, their emotions, their pride and the last thing they would want to do now, is to lose this investment. Why? Because it would mean starting this tiring process all over again, with someone else, who may not be as reasonable as you, who may not even offer what you have offered. So by being prepared to walk away, you can exercise considerable power.

By the way, when it's the other person who walks away, be aware that it may not really be over. They may come back, and very quickly too!

So let's talk about how to frame up your final offer. Let me give you a real life example of how I did this recently.

It was a real estate deal where both sides had invested a great deal of time and energy. We had bartered and moved closer together, but we were still some distance apart. I was buying, and frankly I could still go higher, but I didn't think I really needed to. I was intending to make a final offer and see what would happen. I started by saying:

"Well we have both invested a lot of time and energy in this and we've made a great deal of progress. It would be a real shame, now that we are so close, for all this time and energy to be wasted. We'd have to continue looking — which is not really a problem — we quite enjoy it. Also we're in no great hurry, and there sure is lots around to see, and you, well, you'd have to go through all of this again with someone else. But, because I want to create win/win here, and have us both win, I'm prepared to make one final offer..."Let me make it clear, though, this will be my final offer. Once I make it, we can either take care of the paperwork or I will leave. And I won't be prepared to talk again, not even on the telephone. Is that OK with you? Fine."

With it framed this way, I wrote my offer on a piece of paper, folded it in two, handed it to the other party and said:

"I'll leave you to consider this. I'm going for a coffee next door, come in if you decide to accept and I'll buy you a coffee. If not, I'll say goodbye now. Thank you."

With that I turned, walked to the door, but before I could leave, the wife said: "We'll take it!"

I returned, congratulated them on being tough negotiators, complimented them on getting a fair price and we signed the deal.

Framing it as your final offer is so important and sometimes it can be as simple as: "So let me see if I've got this clear. I make this final concession for you, then you'll be prepared to do this for me. Is that it? Then we'll have a deal? Is that right? Fine, let's do it."

Now some final thoughts on concessions.

Here are four questions which I suggest you ask yourself about all concessions:

➤ What is the real value to the other party here? It could be considerable, remembering that the value they place on something could be vastly different to the value you place on it.

➤ What is the real cost to me here? In reality, it may cost you very little or even nothing at all. For example, asking the bank to settle in 30 days rather than 90 days will cost you nothing if you intend using the property right away.

➤ What do I want in return?

➤ Did I really get it? And what is its real value to me?

Counter Instinctive Negotiating Phase # 6
FINALISING or NAILING DOWN

Several years ago I bought an aeroplane. I did this by buying out four separate shares in this particular aeroplane from four separate individuals, each of whom owned an equal share. As you can imagine this negotiation was complex.

About a week ago, as I was writing this book, an issue came up with one of these previous owners about the purchase and the transfer of ownership. Now, I won't go into detail, but his recollection of what we had agreed all those years ago was different to mine. Has that ever happened to you?

Have you ever concluded a negotiation or perhaps even before final settlement occurred, it all came apart on you? Perhaps your negotiation didn't involve dollars at all, but was simply an agreement for certain actions to be taken by you and the other party, within a certain timeframe, and it just didn't happen. Now when something like this comes apart at the last minute it can be quite a mess! The ill feelings created are sometimes considerable and the amount of time you now need to spend sorting out who agreed to what, can be enormous. In some cases, the damage is even irreparable. The costs in time and money can be extraordinary.

So what can we do to avoid such situations?

When a Deal is not Nailed Down Properly

Well, let me tell you about a friend of mine who has experiences like this happening to her all the time.

In the most recent instance she arranged for the rental of a holiday apartment in an out of state capital city. When she arrived she discovered that the key for the apartment was not available. The owner was expecting her in the afternoon. She had arrived in the morning. She spent most of the day in her car waiting and was furious when he arrived. He was certain she had said afternoon! She gave the owner a cheque and he left.

She was sharing the week's accommodation with two friends and they arrived the following day. When they went to park their cars in the car park of this building, which was beautifully located right in the heart of the city, there were no spaces left for them. She had arranged for three spaces because she knew they would have three cars. She phoned the owner but no answer, and that's the way it was all week. Her friends had to use a nearby public car park, which cost $20 a day for each car, and had to endure the inconvenience of walking and getting their cars in and out. What a headache, but nothing like what was coming her way at the end of the week.

It was time now for her friends to reimburse my friend for their share of the week's accommodation. The rental was $1,400 for the week for this prestigious apartment. They were both sure she had said it was $1,000 for the week. It was originally $1,600 and she had told them she was trying to negotiate it down to $1,000, but she was sure she'd told them that she had finally agreed on $1,400. That was $1,400 to be split three ways — about $467 each. They had been expecting to pay just $333 each, $134 less. Who was right? Who was wrong? And besides, this was supposed to include parking, yet they'd each had to pay nearly $150 more for parking for the week. This was not in the deal, they blamed my friend and tempers flared. Feelings were hurt and it spoilt the week.

As my friend related this tale of woe, I could see that she had not heeded my advice on this last step of the negotiating process, the nailing down agreements phase.

How could she have avoided this disaster?

To answer, let me go back to my original story, the aeroplane situation which had all the hallmarks of becoming a major dispute.

All I had to do was go to my file and there it was. I found my notes on each negotiation with each of the partners, and a copy of the typewritten, signed agreement, which I had prepared all those years ago. I could easily have thrown this "obsolete" paperwork out years earlier, but I hadn't.

I checked the agreement, the payments made, the dates, the addresses and all my notes. Everything was in order. I faxed it to him and it was over. No dispute! No ill feeling! Settled!

Four words sum up my advice on nailing down an agreement after a negotiation: *put it in writing!*

Does this mean that even in the simplest negotiation, you should put everything in writing? In a word... *yes!*

Even if it's not a signed agreement, if you've got your notes to support your understanding of the agreements that you make with people, then in my experience, life will be so much easier if a query arises later on.

On occasions when I've attempted to explain this to my friend with the apartment problem, she's said: "That's OK for you, Mr Negotiator, you're putting together big deals all the time, but I'm not. I'm too busy to put things in writing, I don't have the time!"

"So," I asked, "Do you really have the time to sort out the problems and disputes that I see you getting involved in all the time"?

She responded: "Are you seriously suggesting that this problem with the apartment could have been avoided by me getting an agreement with the landlord in writing?" She asked. "He didn't have such paperwork!"

"Not just the landlord," I responded, "but with your friends too!"

Here's how I would have done it. Once I'd settled on the agreed rental, and what it included, (like three car spaces and the time of my arrival), I would have confirmed my understanding in writing — immediately — and faxed it or mailed it to all the parties involved.

As well as the landlord, I would have done a memo to my two friends confirming the rental rate, what it included, their agreed share, when it was to be paid, etc. Frankly, this memo would have comprised about two sentences and I would have attached a copy of the letter I'd written to the landlord. If I had done it immediately, the whole process would have taken me about five to ten minutes maximum.

The point I'm making here, is that even if you don't have the time, make the time. A few minutes invested early, can save you hours, even days later on. It's as simple as that! It's an important habit to get into and the sign of a real professional too.

On agreements which are more complex and which perhaps involve larger dollars, I always insist on the other party signing the letter, as acknowledgment that they also understand that this is the agreement. Fax it down, have them sign it, fax it back. I'm not sure of the legal standing of a fax in your location, so you might like to check that out, however a signature or initial on a fax or a piece of paper is hard to dispute later when people suffer from "selective amnesia".

By the way, a countersigned letter of confirmation is legally binding and less intimidating than asking the other party to sign a legal agreement properly drawn up by your lawyer. If you do this, of course, they will then want their lawyer to look it over. That lawyer will then want something changed, if for no other reason than to justify their fee, then your lawyer will want to look at it again. The meter on their fees is running, the agreement gets slowed down, and that on its own can sometimes be enough to cause a deal to fall apart or go cold.

So here are a few final thoughts on nailing down agreements:

➢ As much as possible put it in writing
➢ You be the one to put it in writing, simply by saying: "I'll confirm that in writing just to be sure we both understand all the details, OK?" The major advantage of you putting it in writing, is that when you have to sit down and think the agreement through again, step by

step, you may be prompted to recall something you'd forgotten to clarify in your verbal discussion, and you can now include it in the written confirmation and probably get agreement to it. (Part of the reason for this, is that it is in writing, and we'll talk more about why that is so, later on.) The other advantage of you writing up the agreement, is that you can choose the words carefully, to be sure all of your interests are protected. Words are so important, aren't they? Change a word or two in a sentence or paragraph, and you can change the entire meaning or intention of an agreement.

➤ When you confirm, you can confirm every detail, such as the dollars, the date or dates of payment, the location, times, inclusions, exclusions and so on.

➤ You can also build in a default agreement. This is another agreement on what you both agree will happen if one or more of the parties default in some way on the main agreement. This can be very important. What if they don't make a payment on time? What if a wheel does fall off? These things do happen at times. You might as well cover that contingency now to avoid a dispute later on, and in doing so these defaults are less likely to happen.

Part Three

Sources of Power in Every Negotiation

Every time we negotiate we have a feeling of being comfortable or uncomfortable, of being in control or of being controlled. We feel intimidated or feel that we could intimidate the other person (if we choose to). We feel that we have "the upper hand", or we don't.

What controls these feelings during a negotiation? Why do these feelings change and sometimes swing from side to side during a negotiation?

These are feelings of *having* power — and *not* having power — and that's what we're going to take a close look at right now.

(By the way, is power a good thing or a bad thing? I often pose this question to my "live" seminar audiences and get a mixed reaction. Some people say: "Of course power is good", while others feel that power is some "dirty word" conjuring up thoughts, perhaps of dictators like Mussolini and Hitler. My feeling about power is that power, in itself, is neither good nor bad, it's the way that power is used for either good or evil which matters, and that comes down to one's own personal integrity.)

Yes, in a negotiation we can use our power to intimidate, to brutalise, to grind down and to destroy our opponent. Or we can use our power to create positive outcomes and win/win for everyone. The choice is ours.

Where does power come from in a negotiation?

Understanding this question can enable us to feel empowered. Not understanding it, can leave us at the mercy of the other party and their integrity or lack of integrity.

Let's look at a couple of negotiating situations for some answers.

Negotiation 1

It's 1968 and a young man takes control of a Pan Am 747 shortly after take-off from Chicago's O'Hare International Airport. He demands to be flown to the Middle East. He shows the pilot and the command crew of that 747 an elaborate detonator system connected by wires to a vest which he wears. It's crammed with powerful plastic explosives. He's desperate, he's willing to die to have his demands met. He's a member of a ruthless terrorist organisation, known for its activities around the globe. With the release of his grip on the detonator switch, the 747 will be destroyed in an instant, along with the lives of hundreds of innocent passengers.

Now tell me, what would you do as the captain of that 747? What would you do as the head of the negotiating team on the ground, as you monitor the cockpit conversation and listen as this nervous and obviously unstable young martyr shouts obscenities and threats at the crew and passengers? With every moment he is becoming more agitated, more threatening, more dangerous. What would you do?

Let's just freeze-frame on the action for a moment to give us time to think. Something which in real life we may not be able to do in a negotiating situation, right?

So what sources of power are at play here? Perhaps you may even care to take a pen and paper and write your ideas down.

What's happening here?

➢ An obvious source of this individual's power would be the explosives.

➢ Another would be his strong commitment to the outcome. He's prepared to die to win.

➤ The reputation of the organisation to which he belongs — known terrorists who make good their threats — is another source of power.

➤ His physical location in the 747 cockpit, and his isolation in that plane at 37,000 feet over continental USA gives him power.

➤ His unstable and threatening persona give him power ...

....and so the list goes on.

This individual has incredible power. He definitely has the upper hand, wouldn't you say?

Let's switch scenes now to another negotiating situation, a little closer to home, to an everyday negotiation.

Negotiation 2

A young lady, 19 years of age, is shopping for her first car and she and her mother are at the local used car dealership. They have been looking for months for a particular make and model of motor vehicle and a particular colour too. You guessed it, red!

Now she's found just the car she wants. It's perfect in every way, except the price. It's considerably more than what she wants to pay, but it looks so beautiful. She imagines what her friends will say when she picks them up in it. She has just been for a test drive with the salesman and is bubbling with enthusiasm for the car.

"Mum, I really want this car. It's perfect. I love it! And if I get it now, I can take it on holiday next week with Julie and Freda, instead of taking the bus. I've got to have it. I'm so sick of looking. Please won't you and Dad help me with the extra money? I'll pay you back, I promise!"

All of this is being said in front of the very understanding salesman who would really like to sell this car.

Now put yourself in this situation. You're the mother of this young lady. Go ahead now and negotiate a discount with the salesman! Go on, feel empowered, take the upper hand, negotiate hard. I dare you!

But before you can, here comes that salesman's boss:

"John, is this car still available? I've got Roger Smith on the telephone and he's decided to take it. Remember Roger, he was in here yesterday afternoon. He's arranged the finance and would like to come over right away. You haven't sold it have you?"

The salesman looks at you and says: "I'm not sure, has it been sold Mrs Blank?" And now it's your turn to respond. This is the car you've been looking for. Your daughter won't love you any more if you let this "once-in-a-lifetime opportunity" slip away.

What do you say? Go on ask for a discount, I dare you!

So what's happening here? Who has the most power and why? Well, it's obvious, isn't it? The salesman has all of the power.

➤ He has two enthusiastic buyers wanting to pay full price for the car.

➤ You've got time pressures pushing you to make a decision right now. If you don't, you'll lose it and have to start looking all over again. More weekends spent searching and driving to car yards and private sellers. The thought is almost too much to bear.

➤ What about your daughter's disappointment? If you loved her, you'd cough up the extra cash wouldn't you? So your whole reputation as a loving, caring parent is at risk here.

The odds sure are stacked against you, aren't they? Or are they? Let's look for a moment at another factor at play here in both of these negotiating situations.

Needs

Who would you say has the greatest "need" in both of these situations? With the airliner, wouldn't you say that the pilot, the crew, and the ground negotiators have the greatest needs?

➤ They need to save the lives of hundreds of passengers, to say nothing of the millions of dollars that the plane is worth.

➤ They need to be seen to be doing the right thing here, as the eyes of the world are focused on them "live" via CNN satellite TV.

➤ They need to get this thing resolved fast.

The young man on the other hand, seems to have an attitude of "do or die". He'd *like* to have his demands met but doesn't really need them met. He'll be a hero either way. A dead martyr revered for centuries to come, who died for the great cause is a pretty attractive alternative to living the quiet life in the Middle East after his flight gets in. As my friend Herb Cohen would say, *"He cares, but not that much!"*

Let's go back to the car yard again where our intrepid negotiators are poised ready to make a life-changing decision. Who has the greatest need here? The salesman or the mother and daughter? I'd say the mother and daughter, wouldn't you, and by their own open admission? The salesman seems to have very little need to do the deal with them. After all, he has another buyer on the telephone, prepared to pay full price today on this beautiful motor vehicle.

So what's the relationship, I wonder, between NEED and POWER?

It would seem that by examining both of these situations, the party with *highest need* seems to have *lowest power,* while the party with a *lowest need*, seems to have the *highest degree of power.*

HIGH NEED = LOW POWER
LOW NEED = HIGH POWER.

We call this an inverse relationship between need and power. So the major factors affecting our power in a negotiation are our feelings of need, and the perception of our needs by the other party. I purposely chose to say our "feelings" about our needs, because it's our feelings about our needs that are even more important than our actual needs themselves. Our needs are a perception.

Could this whole scenario in the car yard have turned out differently if the mother and daughter had perceived their needs a little differently? If instead of feeling: "I need it. I've got to have it. I've got to have it today or lose out", they felt: "Look, this is a nice car, but there are a lot of nice cars around. There are scores of other car dealers, and it doesn't really matter whether we buy today or next week or next month." Would that have made a difference? You bet it would have. This is another case of where having the attitude of, "I *care,... but not that much!*" is very empowering.

The real truth

Have you ever been in a negotiating situation and wondered what the real truth was about what was happening?

Let's look at our would-be hijacker again. Do you want to know what the real truth was about this situation?

Here's the bottom line. It turned out that our hijacker was a disgruntled university student who had grown up in Chicago. He looked swarthy and a little Middle Eastern, but the heavy accent he used was put on. He was born and raised in America. His girlfriend and he had split up and he wanted to get away from it all. The detonator "switch" which he held in his hand was the spring clamp off a set of jumper leads used to start cars with a flat battery. The wires were connected to a nail pressed into some children's modeling clay, stuffed into the pockets of the outdoor shooters vest which he wore. There were no explosives, no gun, no real weapons at all. He had no connections with any terrorist organisation. He was on drugs and certainly unstable, but could have been easily physically overcome. Yet he wasn't. He had everyone fooled, nearly got away with it and the siege lasted for days.

So did he really have the power? You bet he did, but the power didn't lie in the explosives. It came from the perception of the people around him who attributed him with power he didn't really have.

The point I'm making here is that in any negotiation, *power is a perception*. If others think you have it, even if you haven't really, then you do, indeed, have it. It's all a perception. Consider also: *Power — if you think you have it, you have it!* The reverse is also true: *Power — if you don't think you have it, you don't have it!*

Indeed, I'd like to take my original statement about power being a perception and add a couple of words: *Power is perception is reality!*

Reality, after all, is created by people's perceptions — our own perceptions and those of others. However, the sources of power are very real and I have identified 20 such sources that I'd like to share with you.

Before I do this, would you like to know the truth about the car?

This particular used-car dealership had traded this European car three months ago. Indeed, it was a fairly unique car and there weren't many of them around. Why? Because it was a very unpopular car in this country. It was an enthusiast's car. The type you either love or loath. It was a dog! There had been no interest shown in it for months. It just sat there taking up space. The dealership owner had decided to cut his losses and take almost anything for it, just to get rid of it. He was prepared to take a loss.

And then in walked our enthusiastic mother-and-daughter negotiating team, who simply adored this "dog-of-a-car". They loved it. They needed it, wanted to take it home with them. He couldn't believe his luck. He concocted the story about the other buyer on the telephone and sold it for full price. In reality, he was in high need — higher than the mother and daughter — but they didn't know it. Did he use a "ploy" to get the sale in the end? Yes. Could they have bought it for much less? Yes.

What made the difference was their understanding of power in a negotiating situation. What if the mother and daughter had "cared, but not that much!" and played reluctant buyers, could things have turned out much differently? You bet and we'll be talking more about such ploys in the next part of the book.

Let's look now at 20 sources of power in negotiations. We'll begin with one of the most powerful.

Sources of Power # 1
ATTITUDE

We said before if you *think* you've got power, you've got it. Power is a state of mind. Feeling resourceful and maintaining a resourceful state of mind throughout the negotiation is vital to creating a positive outcome for yourself. If you feel tired, fatigued and unresourceful, don't negotiate. Postpone until you feel more resourceful, more confident. Your attitude plays such a major role.

We've spoke earlier about having the attitude that "Negotiating is just a game!" This is an attitude which can be very empowering. By maintaining a sense of detachment, you can be much more empowered than if you are emotionally involved. Think about that. A "hot head" is often his or her own worst enemy, and sometimes your opponent will do or say things to "suck you in" emotionally. Remember that famous tennis player of the 1980s who would rant and rave on the court at his opponent and the umpires. If his opponent became emotionally involved, it gave him an edge.

So the lesson is remain calm. "I care,.... but not that much!"

Sources of Power # 2
COMMITMENT

Remember our young would-be hijacker? He appeared to be totally committed to his outcome. So much so that he was prepared to die for it. That level of commitment is hard to beat. So it is in any negotiating situation, that the person who is most committed — or at least *appears to be* most committed — will most likely win!

This is a situation where persistency really pays, where sticking to your guns really works. The ability to continue to say "No!" or "I'm sorry, but you'll have to do better than that!" is a trait worth developing. Being prepared to "hang in tough" in the face of reason, adversity, abuse and threats, is incredibly powerful.

We saw this in the Vietnam war, didn't we? For the North Vietnamese the war was their life. It had been going on for a long, long time with the French before the USA ever got involved.

For most Americans and Australians, while the war was important to them, it was really wasn't *as* important. This was a time of much social change in their own countries.

For the North Vietnamese it was a matter of life or death, of survival for their own country. How long were they willing to persist? Forever! Until they won or were wiped off the face of the earth. How long were the Americans prepared to persist? Only until it became the most unpopular war of their glorious history. Until they decided that the war was unwinnable against an enemy who would never relent. So that's the power of commitment and persistence.

```
┌─────────────────────────────────┐
│     Sources of Power # 3         │
│        STRATEGY                  │
│                                  │
└─────────────────────────────────┘
```

We've looked previously at the importance of preparation and understanding the structure of negotiating. The negotiator with a plan or a strategy is very empowered, compared to the negotiator who doesn't know which way is up and which direction to go in next.

By the way, around your strategy, make a decision to stay with the process and leave personal feelings and prejudices out of it. When your opponent becomes emotional, or starts attacking, sit back and say to yourself, "How interesting!" Remain detached. Instead of focusing on people's behaviour, remember to look at people's intentions. *Why* they have said something is much more important than *what* or *how* they have said it.

Remember to separate people from their behaviours. Watch out for ploys, tactics, dirty tricks and stick to the process and your strategy. Don't make the mistake, for example, of thinking it's all over. As someone once said, "It's not over until the fat lady sings!"

Stick to your strategy.

```
┌─────────────────────────────────┐
│     Sources of Power # 4         │
│        LEGITIMACY                │
│                                  │
└─────────────────────────────────┘
```

The power of "legitimacy" comes from anything which validates. For example, what carries more legitimacy, a price quoted out of your head, or showing someone a typed price-list in a bound book? Obviously the typed price-list. This is why retailers use price stickers.

So how do we use this as a source of power? We understand that people will feel we are less flexible if we

97

show them something in writing. That is one reason why I have suggested earlier that offers and agreements be in writing; preferably typed, laminated and bound.

On the other hand, when we are presented with price-tags, agreements, price-lists in writing, we shouldn't allow this to be a source of power for our opponents.

Understand that prices and agreements, even if they are in writing, can be changed. Don't be intimidated. Ask for alterations.

Sources of Power # 5
INFORMATION

It has often been said that information is power (and certainly this seems to be the case in war), and so it is too in a negotiation. The more information you have, the more power you possess. However, don't make the mistake of assuming that all information you have is true. Very often a skilled negotiator will deliberately give misleading information.

The allies used this tactic in World War II to make the D-Day invasion of Europe such an enormous success. They led the German military leaders to believe that they would be coming across the English Channel at its narrowest point into France, when in reality they crossed it at its widest.

So seek out information and question its validity. Never assume anything. Ask questions. Look for explanations. Remember that dumb is smart in negotiating! Ask "How do you mean? Could you please explain that? Is that the best you can do?"

Remember, like the generals who planned D-Day, misleading information given to the other party can be a powerful tool. Watch out for it, and you may care to use this principle yourself, if it's within your integrity and it creates a win/win.

For example, our mother and daughter team, if they had done their market research, could have found out that this was an unpopular model of car. They could have discovered how long it had been sitting on the lot. They could have even found out what the dealer had paid for it. They could have made the dealer aware that they possessed this information and then given lines like, "We're in no hurry, we love looking around, it's fun, we're interested in many different cars, not just this model". If they had taken this approach, they would have been considerably more empowered.

Instead, by revealing the information that they were desperate, this disadvantaged them and empowered the dealer.

Sources of Power # 6
TIME

Time — or the lack of it — is sometimes an incredible source of power in a negotiation. It certainly was at play in our car situation, wasn't it? Both parties had time pressures. However, the mother and daughter revealed their time pressures and the dealer did not. By the way, time is only a perception anyway. How does a deadline get set? Usually a human being has arbitrarily set it. Can deadlines be changed? Of course they can. The "final chance" is rarely the final chance. Negotiating after the deadline does happen. Understanding that deadlines can be extended can be very empowering. Placing deadlines on others can also empower you.

I bought a property recently within hours, and at a very good price, because I told the other party that I had already decided to buy something else the following morning. I made it clear that unless they acted immediately, the opportunity to sell to me would evaporate at 11am the following day. Was this true? Well, yes it was. However the more I compared the two properties, the more I liked their property. If they hadn't conceded to my deadline, I probably would not have bid on the other property. I would have gone back to them after the deadline. Instead, with the pressure of the deadline, the deal was signed at 7pm that night, mainly because I told them that after that I wouldn't be available because I was going to be out to dinner.

So, the lesson here is, avoid being placed in an eleventh hour situation yourself. If you are being pressured, try a "walk away" and see what happens: "Look, that's simply not enough time for me, I'll have to say thanks-but-no-thanks right now, I have plenty of other options", and see what happens. Or alternatively, ask dumb questions like: "Who set this deadline? Why? If the right offer is made, could the deadline be extended?"

A friend of mine negotiates a lot with the Japanese and travels frequently to Japan for this purpose. On his first visit to Japan he was met at the airport by the people he had come to negotiate with. They were just the nicest of people. They had arranged everything for his trip — his accommodation, his return air travel, the lot. Nothing was too much trouble for them. He had set aside three days for the negotiation and was proceeding from Japan to the USA where he was to put together the Japanese component of the project with the American component and then come back to Australia as a hero.

For the first two days of his stay in Osaka he got the red carpet treatment. He was welcomed like a VIP with tours of the plant and meetings with everyone carefully arranged for him. His evenings were full of socialising and building these important relationships. Every time he suggested they start negotiations, he was told that it was not appropriate yet, and so into the third and final day, he was no closer to a negotiated outcome. Time was slipping away, he felt under pressure, he didn't want to offend his hosts, but what could he do? In the end he did conclude the negotiations, but did not get the outcome he was looking for. Guess where those negotiations took place? In the limo on the way to the airport! He had set himself a deadline and revealed what it was to his opponent. This information was useful to the Japanese who are often very skilled negotiators. My friend learnt from this experience. He now leaves time in his schedule to allow for such delays. He even knows the availability of later flights and books alternative accommodation.

Here's a rule to remember about time pressure:

High Time Pressure = Low Power
Low Time Pressure = High Power.

Deadlines are almost always flexible and a skilled negotiator remembers that everything is negotiable — even deadlines.

Investing Time

Another interesting aspect of time as a source of power, is time invested in the negotiation by any party. When buying a car for example, once I've decided exactly which make, model, colour, etc. I want, then it's time to negotiate price. Invariably, I end up buying from a dealer who has invested the most time into the negotiation. Why is that? Is it my sense of fair play? Well, in part it is but sometimes the dealer would probably have been better off not selling to me, but rather keeping that stock to sell to someone else at a better margin. So why do they sell it to me, while other dealers are not prepared to? It's because of the amount of time they have already invested.

You see, when I call another dealer on the telephone and ask him to match or better the deal, I'm just a voice at the end of the telephone. What time has he invested — thirty seconds or maybe a minute? Not a lot. But what if instead of just calling him for a price, I first call him several times with questions on features, options and so on. Then I go in for a demonstration drive and that takes an hour. Then I go back again with some more questions and ask to see his workshop. He or she invests more time with me. Then it's time to introduce him to my wife who takes the same amount of time again. Then I go back with my best friend and ask him to explain it all again. The time and emotion invested is considerable. Will he be more flexible now on the final deal? You bet. He's got so much invested now, he wants to pull something, anything, out of the deal.

As a rule, the more time invested, the more flexible a person is likely to become in a negotiation. Remember this and use this ploy, but watch out for the experienced negotiator who does this to you. I'm not saying don't invest time, just be careful that you are not becoming too emotionally involved for this singular reason.

Sources of Power # 7
RISK

Our would-be-hijacker seemed to have an enormous willingness to take risks, wouldn't you say? Indeed, the greater an individual's willingness to take a risk, the greater their power; the smaller a person's willingness to take a risk, the less power they have.

For example, the employee who is prepared to risk losing his job in order to negotiate an increase in salary, is much more likely to gain the increase than the employee who takes the timid approach and plans to back down if it looks as though they might lose their job by pressing too hard.

If our intrepid mother-and-daughter negotiating team had been prepared to risk walking away from that once-in-a-lifetime deal, their power would have increased.

When your opponent appears to be prepared to take a great risk — indeed risk it all — in the negotiation, be prepared to test that willingness. It may be all bluff. If it is, and you call that bluff, then you remove this source of power.

Playing Chicken

There's a story of a road-train driver who used to play chicken with other road-train drivers just to amuse himself on long hauls across Australia's famous Nullarbor Plain. If you aren't familiar with this route, it is reputed to have some of the country's longest sections of flat, straight road for more than a 1,000 miles. (The road-trains I am talking about are several — sometimes up to ten — semi-trailers hooked up to the one prime-mover. They are an awesome sight thundering along the roads across some the most desolate regions of Australia, often hauling livestock.)

It would seem that this guy had a reputation for being absolutely crazy. Playing chicken is where two of these drivers coming head-on down the middle of the highway towards each other, decide to see who will move over first. If you think about it, it is kind of a negotiation — thundering towards each other at more than 100 km/h. This crazy man would stare blindly ahead, until each driver could clearly see the whites of the other's eyes. He who blinked first invariably would be the first to swerve. This man never lost.

One day, however, a new driver, a wild young man decided that he could beat this crazy man. As he approached, he called him up on his CB radio. There was no response! (CBs were used a lot, which is one of the reasons that this man was so famous. His victories were broadcast for hundreds of kilometres as shaken, defeated drivers who encountered him on the road would curse him on their CB.) He never spoke. It was a part of his strategy, and it worked.

As the two vehicles approached, the young man shouted that he would rather die than chicken out on this duel. Still no response. Then it happened, just as impact seemed inevitable. With a wrenching motion, which the crazy man could see, the young driver thrust the steering wheel of his truck out of the window and held it high in a sign of defiance.

Now that's what I call commitment and willingness to take a risk. With a flick of the wrist he threw the steering wheel into the air. This was too much for the crazy man king of the road who veered at the last minute, avoiding horrible injuries and cursing this new victor.

Now, I'm told this is a true story, but who knows, some of those truck-driver stories can be pretty tall. Some say that what he really threw out was a spare steering wheel, that he'd brought along just for the effect. Pretty effective if you ask me, and a good example of the power you can wield if you are prepared to take risks.

By the way, if you want to make the other party feel more secure and empowered in a negotiation, you may care to do something to minimise the other party's risk, such as offer written guarantees. For example, my company always gives a money-back guarantee on all of its products and services, and I'm certain that we get extra business as a result of this.

> ### Sources of Power # 8
> # OPTIONS AND ALTERNATIVES

You may recall that I spoke earlier about buying some real estate and, after deciding on the property that I wanted, going out purposely to seek alternatives, so I would not have any emotional attachment to this property. Here's the rule:

Lots of alternatives = High power
Few alternatives = Low power.

The secret is to create as many alternative outcomes as you possibly can. This gives you real power. I have known some negotiators to create alternatives out of thin air — figments of their own imagination — which as a "ploy", has given them incredible power. So watch out for negotiators who try to do this. Question them about their alternatives.

Ask them for specifics. You may discover they are bluffing, and once you do, you remove this source of power.

Another way of removing this source of power from the other person when selling, is to make what you are offering unique in some way. Include something which only you can offer, like a service or some specialised knowledge or software. This makes it very difficult for the other party to compare "apples with apples".

Similarly, when you are buying, structure your offer to include components which nobody else can possibly offer. The worst position to be in, is to have no options at all. It's called being "over a barrel".

Sources of Power # 9
WALKING AWAY

We've spoken about this already and obviously the greater our willingness to walk away, the greater our power. The reverse is also true. If we have no willingness to walk away — "But mother, I *must* have it "— then we have very little power. Even if we are not *really* prepared to walk away, *appearing* to be, will give you power.

Remember, power is a perception. Be aware of this, too, with the other person. Somebody who is saying that "I care... but not that much!" may indeed care a great deal, and in reality, not really be prepared to walk away. Again it is useful to test this, as you may find it is just a bluff, and if it is, then you remove an enormous source of power.

By the way, what if you do walk away and they don't try to stop you, or come after you, or call you on the phone? Can you come back? Of course you can (armed with some logical rationalisation) and the only thing that will stop you is pride. Frankly, I have seen people who were only bluffing, but pride stopped them from re-opening the negotiation and everyone lost. Don't let pride cost you. After all it's only a game!

So there two types of walk outs:

➣ **The Hard Walk Out** — This is where you slam the door, abuse the other party and leave for good. I rarely recommend this when you can opt for ...

➣ **The Soft Walk Out** — This is where you withdraw with grace and courtesy: "I really wish we could do something, but we can't so I'll say thank you and good bye!"

Sources of Power # 10
BEING IN RAPPORT

Of course, we've spoken at length about rapport earlier. Being in rapport gives you power. Lack of rapport can remove this power. Sometimes you may choose to be out of rapport with the other party purposely, to remove this possible source of power which they may have. This is why a tactic called "deferring to a higher authority" can work so well. When suddenly you reveal to the other party that someone whom they haven't met, and with whom they have no rapport, is going to make the decision on this, you remove their rapport power.

If I don't want to negotiate something because I've decided that I like it the way it is, I won't even agree to meet or talk to the other party. By now you would realise it's only an opening position. You see, I know that if they meet me, I have to acknowledge that they are a person, and my values system of courtesy, respect and fairness kicks in. I feel compelled to listen, and the more time I invest, the more rapport is built and the more flexible I am likely to become.

Every week I play a negotiating game with the airlines and regardless of what country I'm in, the game seems the same everywhere. When I travel on speaking trips I take special sound equipment, flip charts and sometimes the big heavy metal stands they go on, boxes of cassette programmes, books, etc. In other words, lots of excess baggage. Yet almost without exception, I'm never charged for it. Why? In one word — rapport! Jane, who is General Manager of my company is brilliant at this. She builds such incredible rapport that the subject of excess baggage rarely comes up. The only exceptions for this seem to be when we are running late and Jane and I don't have the time to build this rapport.

So how does Jane do this? Firstly, she smiles at all of the check-in counter staff as she approaches and then selects the one who flashes her the best smile back. She then asks them questions about how their day is going and acknowledges them as a person who has a tough job. She makes them feel important. She jokes with them about baggage and if the question of excess baggage comes up she becomes Detective Columbo — "I'm sorry", she says, "How do you mean excess baggage? What does that mean?" Remember, dumb is smart in negotiating and rapport pays off almost every time. They'll say, "Well I shouldn't, but I'll let it go this time." They simply don't like charging this person who has now built rapport with them.

Sources of Power # 11
COMPETITION

This is a variation on the theme of having options — "If you won't sell it to me with the conditions I need then your competitors will!" Or, "If you don't want to go ahead with this, then I have other people who will!"

Introducing competitors into the negotiation gives you considerable power. Yet I've had clients for whom I've negotiated say to me, "But I don't want to do business with anyone else, I want to do business with them." Well that may be so, but why not introduce some competition as a tool for increasing your power?

I recently saw a computer software supplier slash his prices by more than $8,000 at the very mention that my client had decided to bring in a competitor. Frankly, there was no competitive product which suited my client, but when he "accidentally" scheduled a meeting with each of them, one after the other, so that they passed in reception, the deal suddenly got much better.

If the person you are negotiating with tries this with you, don't be intimidated. If you know that you have some advantage, ask them to clarify their needs and underlying intentions again for you. You know these can't be met by a competitor so then ask them again, if this is an important consideration. In other words *resell* them on doing business with you, but always be careful not to knock competitors.

By the way, introducing a competitive buyer for the car is exactly what the car dealer did in the earlier scenario, and in that case, the competition wasn't even real.

> ## Sources of Power # 12
> ## TITLES

Titles are an interesting source of power. In our culture, and indeed in most cultures, we are impressed by, and in some cases, intimidated by titles. So what are titles really? Just a few letters after or before a person's name. Just a label, yet we sometimes forget this and bestow all sorts of qualities onto a person because of a title. It's true that in some cases, some very real power does come with the title, as in the case of the Queen of England or the Prime Minister of Australia. But with most people with whom we negotiate, these qualities and powers are more imagined, than they are real, and the skilled negotiator knows this.

So you are dealing with the Managing Director of a large company. He or she is still only a human being just like you. People will use their title power if you let them. I delight in being introduced to a big shot who is obviously full of his own importance: "Mr Berry, this is Mr Robert Willingham Cornhauser the Third, Regional Corporate Managing Director." "Great to meet you Bob!" is usually my response.

By the way, there may be some considerable increase in power bestowed upon you, by using a title. If it's appropriate use it. I once had business cards printed for one of my purchasing people which showed him as Director of Operations. His self-esteem went up, and he negotiated better from this new position of strength. Funny what three little words on a business card can do!

Sources of Power # 13
REWARDS AND PUNISHMENTS

There is no doubt about it, if you or the other party (or both) have the ability to reward and/or punish, either or both of you have considerable power, whether you choose to exercise it or not. In most cases, both sides have some of this power.

Our would-be-hijacker appeared to have this power, yet didn't. The mere perception that he did have this power was enough. The Argentinians discovered this during the Falkland Islands war with England more than a decade ago. The British Prime Minister, Mrs Margaret Thatcher told the Argentine President, that Britain had two nuclear powered submarines off the coast of Argentina which would sink any more Argentine ships departing port to head for the Falklands.

The Argentinians feared this awesome power to punish and stayed put. It wasn't until after the war that it was revealed that neither of those two British submarines were even in the Southern Hemisphere at the time.

The threat of this power was enough, and so it is in your negotiating. Don't overlook the power to reward in your negotiations.

I have a friend, who, whenever he's buying anything substantial, asks what the price would be for five or ten and twenty, for example. He infers, and in many cases truthfully, that his company will be buying a multiple. He uses this apparent ability to reward to drive a hard bargain, and then agrees to take just one on trial. Depending upon the performance of that one, and the after-sales service he receives, he may purchase others. Now you may think that is a transparent ploy, but I've got to tell you, he gets incredible deals and amazing after-sales service!

If the deal could get bigger, make sure that the other party knows this. It can give you very real power, if this is important to them.

Sources of Power # 14
CHARISMA

Charismatic power is also a rather interesting source of power and I think we've all seen people who possess it. I have a friend who, for example, has the uncanny ability to have people buy him drinks, meals at restaurants, and even a holiday in one instance, because of his charisma. Just be aware that it exists and be careful that you are not charmed into doing things against your own best interests by a charismatic person.

Examples of such people in history and public life would be, John F. Kennedy, Mahatma Ghandi, President Ronald Reagan and Bob Hawke. Adolf Hitler had it too. You can see it in those old newsreel movies of the huge rallies that he held, particularly prior to the war. President Richard Nixon didn't have it, nor did Prime Minister Paul Keating.

Sources of Power # 15
EXPERTISE

Expertise power is found in individuals who possess, or at least appear to possess, some unique expertise. Our would-be-hijacker was presumed to have some explosives expertise. When we get a plumber in or we see a doctor we bestow on them expertise power.

I recently called a plumber one evening when a pipe burst under our kitchen sink. Water was spraying everywhere and my wife was in a panic. I asked him if he thought he could fix it. He said that he knew he could, and he asked for his call out fee of $95 before he would start. We gave him the cheque and in less than 10 seconds the problem was fixed. I was amazed at his expertise and told him that I thought his $95 fee for less than a minute's work was a bit steep. "That rate is more than $34,000 per hour. Why, I'm a nationally known speaker and author and I don't make that much per hour." "Neither did I," he replied, "when I was a nationally known speaker!"

Actually, that's just my little joke. An oldie but a goodie!

Understand, though, that when you are perceived to have certain expertise, your power goes up considerably. An Australian friend of mine who is a Cadcam designer working with very sophisticated computer-aided design equipment recently returned from a five-year stay in Germany where he worked for BMW, Porsche and Mercedes. He'd been making incredible money in that country but hated the lifestyle.

He was now married and had a little boy whom he wanted to grow up in Australia. His big fear was that he could not earn the money that he could make in Germany.

After all, he knew what the industry rate per hour was in Australia, and there was no comparison. I told him to consider asking at least double those rates. Why? Because he had expertise that people would be prepared to pay a premium for. He just had to mention names like BMW and Porsche, and his new exorbitant rate, and doors opened for him, which I'm sure would not have had he been asking the same fee as everyone else.

Sources of Power # 16
ENVIRONMENT

The environment in which you negotiate can have a major impact on negotiations. Such factors as its location, its lighting, its privacy — or lack of it — noise levels, temperature and so on, will either empower or disempower you, or the other party. Also check to see how many people will be attending and don't be intimidated if you are out-numbered. Seating can also be important. Sitting at a large table is different to sitting at a small one. Check it all out in advance.

Also, negotiating on the other party's "home turf" can give that party tremendous confidence, and may, if you let it, intimidate you. After all, he is surrounded by familiar faces and symbols of power. On the other hand, you may *want* the other party to feel relaxed and comfortable. Just be aware of the power that the environment creates.

By the way, much of this occurs at an unconscious level. Several years ago I was invited from Melbourne to far north Queensland to negotiate with a company in that area. I arrived at the meeting in the clothes I was wearing when I left Melbourne on a cold winter day. My clothing was totally inappropriate for their climate. I loosened my tie as we travelled to the site chosen by them for the negotiation — a stuffy hotel room with no air-conditioning. The humidity was incredible, sweat poured off everyone. I suspected that this was a ploy and I suggested a 10 minute break. During the break I changed into comfortable cool clothing and announced how nice it was to be back to the hot weather of Queensland where I had grown up. That afternoon they switched hotels and we were in air- conditioned rooms for the rest of the talks.

Another example of how the environment can be used as a source of power, involves a female relative of mine who had a propensity for becoming loud and aggressive, and had a tendency to hit me as we negotiated. Frankly, it more than annoyed me. It hurt me, and it would end in no positive outcome for either of us. I switched all meetings from a private place to a public place, such as a restaurant, and the behaviour stopped. We finally started making progress.

Choose an environment that suits you. If you don't get what you need, negotiate for it before the real negotiations begin.

Sources of Power # 17
HEALTH AND WELL-BEING

It almost goes without saying, doesn't it, that we don't engage in risky activities like sky-diving, scuba diving, using dangerous machinery — and negotiating — when we are feeling fatigued or ill. It is also unwise to negotiate if you are unwell. Arrange to have the meeting rescheduled or have someone else negotiate for you.

During negotiations choose your own food and drinks. You don't have to settle for what is provided. Eat well, get adequate rest and drink lots of water. There is no doubt that some people become more flexible as they grow fatigued, whereas others simply become more aggressive and angry. Judge for yourself in every situation, but be aware of the power tiredness has to influence people. Military and police interrogators understand this only too well, don't they?

```
┌─────────────────────────────────┐
│                                 │
│     Sources of Power # 18       │
│          SITUATION              │
│                                 │
└─────────────────────────────────┘
```

This power usually comes as a direct result of the particular situation a person is in. For example, our hijacker was somewhat inaccessible in that cockpit of the 747, at 37,000 feet, wasn't he?

Another example of situational power can be seen in some banks and post offices. You're standing waiting in line. The line moves slowly because the person behind the counter is having a private conversation about their date last night. You finally arrive and they put up a sign, "Closed For Lunch". Don't laugh, it still happens in some places.

I was in a bank about a year ago, when the accountant of that branch was exercising his situational power over me. He was being condescending, as he filled in the wrong set of forms and then blamed me. He grumbled as he started slowly to fill in the new set.

So what can you do? Well, you can simply accept it and not be intimidated. This removes their power. Or you can do what I did, which, frankly, I don't recommend. It nearly got me arrested as the security man who was stationed outside came in to see what was happening. I simply started to question this man's authority, I asked for the manager, I criticised his bad attitude and his lack of good service. Why would this nearly get me arrested? I did so in a very, very, loud screaming voice and then exited the bank. I've been back once since, to close all accounts, and yes, he was there again, and yes, everyone did remember me. Service was much better on that occasion!

Sources of Power # 19
REFERENT POWER

Referent power is the power which comes from having a consistent set of values. President Ronald Reagan had it, Bill Clinton did not, particularly during the early part of his term in office. Do you remember how he vacillated on issues? First he said yes, then he said no. He went to and fro and lost a great deal of the respect people had for him.

With Reagan, people didn't always like his policies but they knew that if he said something, he meant it, and there would be no changing his mind. They could count on it. People like the security of dealing with someone who has a consistent set of values, who is not likely to change their mind after the negotiation. It gives you power, whether they like what you say or not. You get it by being straight and consistent with the people you deal with.

Sources of Power # 20
UNPREDICTABILITY

Unpredictability is not the opposite to referent power. It's just that if you are predictable all the time, you can very easily become shark bait!

I believe I gave you a good example of this earlier on, as to how my predictable, Mr-Nice-Guy behaviour, made me an easy target to be out-negotiated.

Don't always be predictable. Practise being unpredictable at times in your negotiations. Sometimes disagree on issues that the other party thinks you will agree on. If the other party behaves in an unpredictable manner, don't be intimidated. After all, it's only a game!

Here's a final thought to wrap up this subject of power. Remember that *power is a perception.*

If you think you've got it, you've got it. If you don't think you've got it, you don't have it!

Part Four

Ploys, Gambits And
Dirty Tricks

Right throughout this book in many of the stories I have related, you may have noticed some ploys or some negotiating gambits, or what you may even have decided to call, "dirty tricks".

Do people actually use these in negotiating?

Of course they do!

Are they right to use them?

Well, that's a judgement that you will have to make, but the fact is they are used.

Should you use them?

Well again, that's a question that only you can answer from your perspective of integrity.

The point I'm making here, is that they do get used, and if they are going to be used, particularly against you, then it would be a good idea to know how to recognise them. Then, if you can understand what's happening, perhaps you can counter them.

I'm also going to suggest that these ploys are really neither good nor bad. They are simply tools that can be used to create win/lose outcomes, or to create positive outcomes — win/win — for both you and the other party. The choice as to how you use these tools is entirely yours.

Difference between Ploys, Gambits and Dirty Tricks

So what's difference between a ploy, a gambit and a dirty trick? I've heard it said that a ploy or a gambit is something that we do, while a dirty trick is something that gets done to us!

To understand these ploys, I've decided that we should visit some fairly typical — and some not so typical — negotiating situations, and sit in on these, to observe some negotiations as they happen. Then we are going to ask the question, "So what happened"? and see what we can learn from each situation. You are probably already very familiar with many of these situations. You've seen them happen before. It's just that up until now, you may not have realised what was happening. This time you'll have an opportunity to gain some valuable distinctions, and as I believe we've said before.....*clarity leads to power*..... particularly in negotiating!

Negotiating Ploy # 1
THE NIBBLE

Come with me now, as we go to a fairly typical retail scene. It's a busy appliance store, and the salesperson is speaking.

Sales Person: So with all the features we've discussed, that will be $1,595.

Customer: That's not bad. In fact, that's better than I thought.

Sales Person: Plus, of course, $50 delivery and $100 installation.

So what's happening here? This sales person is using a technique that we've spoken about before. It's called the *Nibble.* The lesson here? If you are the customer, never say yes too quickly. It encourages nibbling. A better response would have been to play the *Reluctant Buyer.* This brings us to another ploy. Here's an example:

Sales Person: So with all the features we've discussed, that will be $1,595.

Customer: I'm not sure. That's more than I expected.

If, on the other hand, you are the sales person, the nibble can be a very valuable technique used in conjunction with what we call in NLP terms, *calibration*.

(Calibration simply means observing the visual, auditory and kinesthetic — that is physical reactions or responses — to what you have just said, shown or done. By the way, if you are experienced in NLP, you'll recognise that calibration is much more than this, but for now, this is sufficient explanation.)

Based on what you have observed, you may then care to nibble for a little more, as our sales person in this situation just did. So the lesson when you are asking for something, such as an asking price, is to chunk your offer into several parts. If you get a positive response to the first chunk, add another chunk.

Let me give you an example:

Sales Person: Plus, of course, $50 delivery......

Check the response.

Sales Person: ...... and $100 installation.

People often become stressed just before a decision is made, but once it has been made the mind then seeks to confirm that this original decision was a good one. So the sales person is now much more likely to get a positive "yes" to the delivery and installation fees than if they had mentioned them up front.

Let's move now to another scenario. It's one with which, if you have teenagers in your family, you may be very familiar. Or perhaps you may have done this yourself as a teenager.

Teenager: Hey, Mum can I borrow the car tonight?
Parent: Well, yes, I suppose so. (Reluctantly)
Teenager: Some extra cash for petrol would be handy...
Parent: All right, I suppose so. (Hands over some cash.)
Teenager: ...and for parking?

Parent:	OK. (More cash.)
Teenager:	...and for something to eat after the show?
Parent:	All right then but be home by midnight. (Even more cash.)
Teenager:	How about 1am?

We've seen some pretty good nibbling there, haven't we? Have you noticed how good kids are at negotiating, and they haven't even done a course on it!

Let's return to that original retail situation and see how a customer who understands nibbling might approach this same situation.

Sales Person:	So with all the features we've discussed, that will be ....$1,595......
Customer:	Fine. I'll take it. Of course that does include delivery and installation, doesn't it?
Sales Person:	Well, no it doesn't...... but I suppose I could arrange that for you.
Customer:	Fair enough!

Here we see the customer using the nibble very effectively. The lesson is not to make all of our demands up front. Sometimes it's better to wait until the negotiation is over, and then go back for more.

The sales person in this case is psychologically vulnerable immediately after he feels that the sale has been made. Why? Because he doesn't want it to all come apart now, not after all the time and effort he has invested. In his mind, all the struggle and tension is over. Whew! He doesn't really want to start negotiating and stressing out all over again. Not when it's so much easier to just say "yes".

So in summary, the principle of nibbling says that you can often get a little bit more, even after everything has been agreed. Car dealers know this so well, don't they? They know that customers will negotiate very hard on the car itself, and when it's all over, they'll ask whether they would like to include fabric protection, a security system, a better hi-fi sound system, metallic paint, rust protection and so on. And if we are not careful, we find ourselves saying,

"Well OK then, why not!" and before you know it, we've just added another $2,000 to the car's price, and guess where the profit for the dealer often is? That's right, in these add- ons, at the end, when all the negotiating is over!

On a BMW I bought about a year ago, I finally knew it was going a little too far when they wanted more than $1,000 for a tow bar! I said no, and had one put on later for less than $400.

So nibbling can be a pretty effective ploy.

The Counter Gambit for the Nibble

If it is so effective, what can we do to counter such a ploy, if somebody uses it on us?

Let's return to that last retail situation, where the customer is a skilled negotiator and has just nibbled.

Sales Person: So with all the features we've discussed, that will be ....$1,595.

Customer: Fine. I'll take it. Of course, that includes delivery and installation doesn't it?"

Sales Person: Oh come on now, you've negotiated a fantastic price here, don't make me throw in that too! Fair enough?

Here we see the sales person using a very effective counter gambit to the nibble. It is designed to stop this grinding down process. One of the most effective methods of countering the nibble is to subtly make the other person feel cheap. Just smile and say: "Come on now, John, you've got yourself a wonderful deal here, don't make me throw that in too!"

By the way, if they had brought this up earlier, we would have, as skilled negotiators, asked for something in return, wouldn't we? So if they still persist with the nibble, suggest that if they really want this too, we need to re-open the negotiations and this time include what they are asking for now, and of course that may change some of the things we have already agreed on. This is normally sufficient to counter a persistent nibbler.

```
Negotiating Ploy # 2
THE FLINCH
```

Another ploy that we have spoken about a lot is the *flinch*. Let's return to that original retail situation again and listen as the customer really plays the reluctant buyer and uses the flinch.

Sales Person: So with all the features we've discussed, that will be .... $1,595.

Customer: How.... much!!!! $1,500!!!! That's a lot of money!" (recoiling in horror!)

The "flinch" can be used very effectively to lower the other party's expectations. What often may follow here now, is a concession.

Sales Person: Of course that does include delivery and installation.

Customer: That's still a lot of money!

Sales Person: And I could probably arrange to include some supplies too!

The principle of flinching says that you should visibly react whenever a proposal is made to you. People are watching for your reaction. Again in NLP-speak this is "calibration".

If, for example, they make you a low offer and you don't flinch, they are probably entitled to assume that this low offer is still within your negotiating range, and that you will accept it. Maybe you are happy with it, and you could even accept it. However, if you accept it without flinching, you may be missing an opportunity to do much better. Also if you don't flinch, it sets up the response from the other person of, "I could have done better than that!" Then they don't feel good about the outcome, even though they did negotiate you down from your original position.

> # Negotiating Ploy # 3
> # THE HIGHER AUTHORITY

Let's look now, at another situation which is about to become a negotiation. Someone is picking up a vacuum cleaner which has been in for repair.

Customer: Look I'm not at all happy about the charges for this repair. It's too much for what you've done. I'm not prepared to pay that much!

Repairer: Hey, I only work here. If you don't pay the full amount, you can't take the goods. I couldn't possibly authorise any change to this invoice.

Have you ever been in a situation like this? Now, perhaps our repair counter manager can't negotiate a reduction, or perhaps he can. Maybe he's even the owner of the business, but he's not saying. If this is the case, he's using a very powerful ploy called the Higher Authority Gambit.

Using this gambit he is avoiding being pressured to make a decision, or to make a concession. The lesson here in negotiating is that even if you do have full authority, it's often useful to say that you haven't, or indeed to organise it so you really don't have full authority.

So what can our agitated customer do now to counter this ploy?

The Counter Gambit

Customer: Look I'm not at all happy about the charges for this repair. It's too much for what you've done. I'm not prepared to pay that much!

Repairer: Hey, I only work here. If you don't pay the full amount you can't take the goods. I couldn't possibly authorise any change to this invoice.

Customer: So who could authorise a change?

That's a very effective counter gambit. Find out who can make the decision, and then ask to speak to that person. But there is a counter, to this counter gambit.

To counter such a request, it is better to have some faceless group as your higher authority, rather than an individual. Individuals can be contacted, however, if your higher authority is a group of people, like a management committee, or the board of directors, we all know how difficult it can be to get a group together in the one place, at the one time, to decide on anything, don't we?

Whenever I'm negotiating, as much as possible, I never have full authority. It gives me time to think, to consider options, and it allows me to play another game that we'll look at later.

So, is there a way to avoid this higher authority gambit being used on you?

Well, not always, but a very good way of minimising the event of this happening comes out of one of the very early steps we discussed in our negotiating model. That's the Gathering Information Phase, where we ask about decision-makers. For example, "If this proposal exactly met your needs, is there any reason why you couldn't make a decision on this today?" If there is a higher authority, we'll find out now, and if there is, it's wise to find out early who they are, and try to involve them early.

Negotiating Ploy # 4
THE BOTTOM LINE

Let's go now to a computer dealership as a sales person concludes her presentation:

Sales Person: Well, it's a beauty isn't it? Sorry it took so long to show you everything, but there's so much to consider.

Customer: Well, I really appreciate all the time you've spent with me, and all the work you've put in, but it's just not what I'm looking for. I'll probably end up with something much smaller, I just don't need everything that yours has.....

(The client stands up and closes his briefcase.)

But to be fair to you... what's the very lowest price you would take for this computer?

So what's happening here? The customer has had the sales person invest a great deal of their time, energy and emotions into this presentation and then says, sorry, this is not really what I want.

How would you feel if you were the sales person right now? Pretty deflated and disappointed, right? After all the time you've invested, it's all over and you are about to come out of this whole thing empty-handed. You haven't even had a chance to negotiate. Or have you? This is what an unskilled negotiator might be led to believe by a skilled negotiator, which this potential customer appears to be.

As he said this, he stood up closed his briefcase and prepared to leave. I've even seen a skilled negotiator walk to the door and with one hand on the door knob, pause and say:

Customer: But to be fair to you... what's the very lowest price you would take for this computer?

He's being so kind now, isn't he? "But to be fair" he says, and then asks for your lowest price. If the sales person is not careful now, she'll find herself giving an enormous price concession, believing that it's all over and she has nothing to lose, when in fact it's not all over. In reality, it is just beginning and they've just "bottom-lined" the deal. Indeed, the customer has just used a ploy called The Bottom Line Gambit.

The negotiating hasn't even begun in earnest, yet they've succeeded in making the sales person give a major concession already. Now it may not be their bottom line yet, but they've probably moved a long way towards it.

Then the customer pauses, comes back, sits down and probably says something like: "Well, maybe I'm being too hasty. Tell me again what I'm getting for that price?" and then the real negotiations begin. Watch out for this one. It's very effective.

Negotiating Ploy # 5
THE VICE

Let's move to another negotiating scene. It's a retail carpet showroom. The customer has been looking around and knows that the price they are likely to get here is going to be very, very good.

Sales Person: Well, our best price on this is $13,500.

The customer is surprised. It's less than what they were expecting, but being a skilled negotiator, playing reluctant buyer, they respond with....

Customer: How much? (Startled and shocked.) I'm sorry, you'll have to do better than that!

We call this The Vice Gambit. No matter how good the offer, the vice works amazingly well to get an even better price, almost every time. Indeed, using it may cause the sales person in this case to reveal their bottom line right away. But of course there is a counter gambit for the vice:

Sales Person   Exactly how much better than that will I have to do?

This will nail down the concession expected by the customer and prevent the sales person offering too great a concession.

Negotiating Ploy # 6
GOOD GUY/BAD GUY

Let's move now to a real estate office. A sales person is sitting down with the owner of a property and a prospective buyer. We join the scene as the owner says to the sales person:

Owner: Look I'm sorry, I'm not going to waste any more time on this. I've got another meeting to go to. I don't think they're really serious about making us a sensible offer. Goodbye.

With this he gets up and walks out, slamming the door behind him.

Sales Person: I'm sorry, he gets that way sometimes. He's so difficult to deal with and I'd really like to see you get this property too. Hey, I've got an idea. Why don't you let me see what I can do for you with him?"

Buyer: Well, what do you think you can get him to go along with?

Have you ever been placed in this position? If you were the prospective buyer here, and if you were not a skilled negotiator and didn't understand what was happening, you might find yourself asking the sales person to negotiate with the buyer on your behalf, and he or she is not even on your side!

I found myself in exactly this situation recently with a friend who was buying a house, and my friend said this: "So what do you think they might go along with?" This gambit is called Good Guy/Bad Guy Gambit. It's an oldie but a goodie, and gets its name from those old police shows shown on late night TV these days. You've seen them — there is a good cop and a bad cop and the suspect is brought in for interrogation. The first cop is always the nice guy. He offers coffee, and is caring. The second cop is the tough, mean guy. He threatens the suspect with harsh language, even physical violence, and is restrained by the good cop. Then suddenly, he's called away to the telephone in another room. The first cop then offers the suspect a cigarette and tries to assure him that everything will be all right. He's concerned, though, as he has seen the other cop really lose his temper with another suspect in this very same room, and it wasn't a pretty sight. And while the suspect is now squirming with apprehension, he makes him an offer: "Hey, why don't you tell me what you know and I'll see what I can do with him for you". And before you know it, the suspect has opened up and is telling this good cop, everything he knows.

Now, if you don't recognise what they are doing to you, it can be a real temptation to believe that the good guy is on your side, when of course, he or she is not!

By the way, President Jimmy Carter and President Elect, Ronald Reagan played this game on a global scale during the Iranian Hostage Crisis in the 1980s. Do you remember what happened? Carter was the nice guy. He suggested that the hostages be released before Reagan took office. He said: "Hey, if you don't like dealing with me, you are going to like this Reagan guy even less. He's crazy. He's tough. He won't hesitate to use force."

Now perhaps the Iranians even did some market research on Reagan and got a hold of some of his old cowboy movies, because do you remember what happened? The hostages were released on the very morning of Reagan's inauguration, showing that these tactics do really work.

Now is there a counter gambit for the good guy/bad guy ploy? To answer this, let's return to that same scene in the real estate office and see how a skilled negotiator might handle this situation.

Owner: Look I'm sorry, I'm not going to waste any
              more time on this. I've got another meeting

to go to. I don't think they're really serious about making us a sensible offer. Goodbye.

Buyer: Hey, come on you two, you're not going to try that good guy/bad guy stuff on me are you? Look, you want to sell the property, I want to buy the property, why don't we all sit down and see what we can work out that's fair to all of us, OK?

The best way of dealing with this ploy is to simply tell them that you see that it's just a ploy. There's a saying I like to use about ploys: a ploy perceived is no ploy at all!

And this goes for all ploys. Once you recognise and expose a ploy, you take away its power.

**Negotiating Ploy # 7
THE SET ASIDE**

Let's move now to the purchasing office of a large corporation where the purchasing manager is talking to a printer's representative. The meeting has just started and the manager begins with:

Manager: Look, we only do business with companies that give us 60 days trading terms. If you can't do that, there's no point in discussing this any further.

Now if the sales person is not careful, this negotiation will reach an impasse and stall even before it has begun; before sufficient momentum has developed; before a relationship has been established; before enough time has been invested; before all of the factors have been considered. An inexperienced negotiator will either give a concession — possibly unnecessarily — or lose the whole negotiation before it even starts.

So what could this sales person do?

The solution lies in the set aside gambit:

Manager: Look, we only do business with companies that give us 60 days trading terms. If you can't do that, there's no point in discussing this any further.

Sales Person: Let's just set that aside for a moment and see what else is important to both of us. Fair enough?

And I suggest that as this is being said, we gesture with our hands, particularly for the visual and kinesthetic types, and pick up this issue (invisibly) from the table and set it aside, on say the edge of the desk.

I was negotiating with an elderly Chinese gentleman once and used this gesturing process so well, that he immediately got up from his side of the desk and came around to my side so he could pick up this invisible issue which I'd just set to one side. He then put it squarely back in the centre of the desk again, saying: "No Mr Berry, we need to leave here on desk and talk about this now." I stood up, picked up this invisible issue again, and this time placed it on a small table behind me, asking again, if we could just set this aside for the moment. He, again, came around to my side and picked up this invisible issue and placed it again, back on the desk: "No, Mr Berry, I insist, we need to leave here on desk and talk now." Again I picked up this invisible issue and this time I stood on my chair and placed it on top of the bookcase behind me. He again stood up, came around my side, but this time, because I was now sitting on the chair, couldn't reach to where I had placed this issue, to set it to one side. "No, Mr Berry, we really need to have it on desk now". And there was nothing there at all! After a few seconds, though, trying to figure what to do, he stopped and said: "Well, OK then, but we must get down off top shelf before you leave today"! It's a funny story, but it really does demonstrate the power of this technique, doesn't it?

Negotiating Ploy # 8
THE HOT POTATO

Let's move now to another real estate situation and of course it could be any product or issue really. The prospective buyer says:

Buyer: But I have a budget of just $250,000.

or he might say:

Buyer: But the problem I have is.....

We call this passing the hot potato and it occurs fairly frequently in negotiations where one party has a problem and wants the other party to be responsible for it — to own it. The problem is that an unskilled negotiator may just buy into this problem, and before they know it, it becomes their problem. Have you ever done this? I know I have.

Let's see how a skilled negotiator might handle this hot potato gambit:

Buyer: But I have a budget of just $250,000.

Sales Person: Fine, I understand, but if I find a property which meets your needs and it's just outside your budget, should I show it to you, or only show it to my other buyers?

Our purpose here is to test the validity of this opening position. Another example might be:

Person A: But it's not in the budget!

Person B: So, who set this budget and who has the authority to change the budget?

This counter gambit forces the other party to own the problem and really tests the validity of the comment. Often, you'll find it is not a valid comment at all. Their purpose was to seek a response from you.

Negotiating Ploy # 9
SPLITTING THE DIFFERENCE

Let's look now at a process which is sometimes called splitting the difference. I'm sure you've probably heard this expression before. You've perhaps even seen it done before, where two people are negotiating and they are a number of dollars apart, so they end up splitting the difference and they meet half way.

The process I'm about to show you, if it is done right, can have you meeting at 25/75 in your favour, rather than 50/50, and it will still allow the other party to feel that they have won. The secret to using this technique is to have the other party suggest that you split the difference, rather than you suggesting it yourself. This can take real skill. Let's look at how it might sound coming from a highly skilled Top Gun negotiator:

Top Gun: So you want $9,000 for this car and my budget only stretches to $8,000. What a shame we can't get together on this when we are only $1,000 apart....It's a real shame... I wonder what we could do? (Pause and wait...wait...wait...)

Seller: Well, I want to see you get this car too. (He sighs.) Tell you what, why don't we split the difference?

Top Gun: How do you mean? Do you mean you're saying $9,000 and I'm saying $8,000, so let's agree on $8,500. Is that what you're saying?

Seller: Yeah, I suppose so. Hey, why not?

Top Gun: Sounds fair to me. Hopefully we can get together at that. I'll have to check with my wife first though. May I use your telephone?

Let's stop the action there and ask what's happening?

Well firstly our Top Gun negotiator has had the other party suggest that they split the difference, and then he has deferred to a higher authority, his wife. Why?

Let's see how that telephone call went. Maybe we'll find the answer there:

Top Gun: Well, I really tried, but I'm sorry, she said not a cent above $8,000. What a shame... what a shame...... and we're only $500 apart.

Stop! Did you hear what he said? Now we are only $500 apart! What happened to the $1000? Let's see what the seller's response may be.

Seller: Well, I tell you what, why don't we split the difference on that $500. Do you think she'll go for that?

Top Gun: So what you're saying is that you'll agree to $8,250, is that what you're saying?

Seller: Yeah, why not? Do you think you can get her to go for it?

So do you see what happened? We also have a game of Good Guy/Bad Guy going on here, too. The skill is in encouraging the other party to suggest this splitting of the difference.

Negotiating Ploy # 10
THE TRADE OFF

Let's look now at something we came across earlier in the Bartering Phase of our negotiating model. Here's the sales manager of a company getting some bad news (or is it good news?) from their printer.

Printer: Hey, you know those brochures you needed by the 10th, we've had a problem here and it's going to be more like the 20th. I'm sorry, I've done everything I can. I hope that will still be OK, Bob.

So what would the average person say now in response? "Well I suppose it will have to do." Or, "That's OK, we don't need them right away, we still have some of the old ones left. Sure the 20th will be fine!"

What would a Top Gun negotiator say in response? Do you see that this is not just the delivery of some information, it's really an opportunity to negotiate with this printer. After all, they are negotiating a shift in delivery date with you. What did you learn in the Bartering Phase? When you are asked for a concession, ask for something in exchange. It stops the grinding down process, and you may get something in return and it could stop this happening again in the future.

Let's see how our skilled negotiator handles this:

Top Gun: Well, I'm not sure. I think they had a deadline on this. I'll try to see what I can do with them for you. But, if I can do this for you what can you do for me? (Pause and wait... wait...)

Printer: Well, I don't know. I tell you what, what if we ran 1,000 extra for you at no cost, would that help?

Sure, why not? Or you might get a discount. Or even if you get nothing in return, it may give you a bargaining chip in a future negotiation: "Remember when you were late with that brochure job, Fred, and I convinced them to wait another ten days. Well, I tell you what, I need a favour now. I have a rush job, can you help me?"

**Negotiating Ploy # 11
FUNNY MONEY**

Let's move the scene now to a new car dealership. Our negotiator has done a fabulous job of negotiating a great deal on a car. It's the base model, but what the heck, it's a good deal and who needs those extras anyway?

Sales Person: You know, you've made a great decision
to take this car. Congratulations! I'll write
it up for the lease company for you. By
the way, just before I do, did you know
that for just an extra $3 a day you could
enjoy the luxury version, with all those
extras you liked so much. How about it?
Your comfort is worth $3, isn't it?

Boy it's tempting to say yes, isn't it? Particularly when it's
put that way. But be careful, if our buyer says yes, he's just
agreed to spend an additional $5,475, on a five year lease
in just 30 seconds. We call this negotiating with Funny
Money. Sales people use it a lot. Why? Because it works!

```
┌─────────────────────────────────────┐
│        Negotiating Ploy # 12         │
│          THE WALK AWAY               │
└─────────────────────────────────────┘
```

The next one we have already spoken at length about.
It's called the The Walk Away gambit. Once you pass the
point where you are saying to yourself, "I'm not prepared
to walk away from this. I've got to have it". You lose a
great deal of your power in the negotiation.

There's no such thing as a once-in-a-lifetime deal, when
you're buying that beautiful car, or that piece of real estate,
or negotiating that new job. I've got a saying: "Good deals
are like trams, if you miss one, there will eventually be
another one along, just as good, maybe even better."

It pays to be patient! It's counter-instinctive again, but it
doesn't pay, or should I say it can be very costly, to become
so emotionally involved that negotiating stops being a
game, and you just can't walk away.

When my daughter, Skye, was a baby, her mother and I
attended a school fete. They had one of those auctions to
raise funds. We had spotted a bright yellow, fibre glass,
slippery slide there that we knew would be a part of this

auction. I said to my wife: "Watch the Master later. We're taking that home for a song."

The time for the auction came. I opened the bidding low, a few other people bid and then dropped out. All except for this lady across the other side of the crowd. She bid, I bid higher. I bid higher, she topped me, and so it went on. In the end I did get the slide. It was a real master stroke. The great negotiator had won another victory, and it only cost me twice what the slide was worth. That's right. I'd paid double its value.

I found out afterwards that the lady bidding against me had promised her son too. We both had a good laugh about our foolishness, but this was a classic example of where walking away would have been the best option.

Have you ever been shopping in a market? They are great places to practise negotiating. Frankly, I don't like shopping, but years ago I let my friends and relatives take me to markets shopping with them, just so I could practise my negotiating skills.

This is when I discovered the real power you can have if you are prepared to walk away.

My friends would choose an item they wanted — say a leather jacket — and then I'd start to negotiate on their behalf, not letting the other person know that I wasn't buying for myself. I didn't care whether we bought or not. After all, it wasn't for me, so I could be very unemotional. I'd make them an offer, and then begin to walk away. So they'd come walking after me. It was a great game, and a real learning experience for me.

A couple of years ago in Tijuana, Mexico, I was in a shop and was told: "Sorry, that's the best deal you'll get anywhere Señor!" As I started to walk out the door, the man came out of the shop and followed me down the street. The further away from his shop we got, the better the deal became.

You have real power if you are prepared to walk away. Practise walking away.

136

Negotiating Ploy # 13
DELAYING AND STALLING

The next ploy is again something that we've talked about before — Delaying and Stalling.

Sometimes people will delay and stall hoping to put you under time pressure at the end. They'll drag out meetings and indulge in lots of small talk. They'll set up meetings and cancel them at the last moment. They'll go around and round in circles, take long meal breaks, and so on. Anything to stall. If you suspect this is happening, rather than looking at the behaviour, look at what their intention might be behind the stalling. Do they hope to outlast you and wear you down, so you give up, or become more flexible? Are they trying to frustrate you and drive you crazy? If so why? Look objectively and remain detached, if it is starting to get to you. Make arrangements in advance so that there is no deadline on you, if this is possible.

Very often deadlines are self-imposed. Don't do this to yourself! If you suspect the other party is using this tactic, there are a couple of things you can do. Firstly, you can suggest to them that you know what they are doing, and it won't work! Tell them why. Alternatively, or as well, consider giving *them* a deadline for the conclusion of the negotiations or for various phases of it. Make sure that this deadline is well within any real deadline that you may have.

Negotiating Ploy # 14
THE PRE-CONDITION

The next one I'd like to look at with you is called the the Pre-Condition Tactic. This is where a negotiator gains concessions from someone, in return for simply considering to negotiate at all. Ridiculous? Well, yes, you're right, but it happens. It can be a very tricky tactic, and if you're on the receiving end you can find yourself giving concessions when the negotiation hasn't even started.

For example, if somebody says something like: "Look if you're prepared to make me your sole distributor for this region, then and only then, am I prepared to start talking with you." This is the Pre-Condition Tactic. In this situation, if you're not careful, you can find yourself agreeing to limit your distribution, your sales and even your options for other buyers, all before the negotiation has really even started. If you were going to consider such a concession, it should be at the Bartering Phase of the negotiation, where if you did concede, you would trade it for something you wanted.

The counter gambit for this is to simply start negotiating anyway, and ask for something in return. Alternatively, use the Set Aside Gambit to enable the negotiation to gather some momentum, and gain some time and emotional commitment from the other party.

Negotiating Ploy # 15
PERSONAL ATTACKS

This next one we have also discussed earlier, but I'd like to remind you that it is a tactic. It's the tactic of using Personal Attacks. A personal attack may be made on purpose to put you off balance and make you emotional. Remember, we are creatures of emotion and when we are emotional, we sometimes say, or do, or agree to things which in a calm rational state of mind, we would never have considered.

So watch out for this tactic.

The counter tactic is to simply remain unemotional, detached and not to take it personally.

Simply recognising that it might be a tactic, will bring a smile to your face and act as a "pattern interrupt". It will stop you from responding in an instinctive manner and maybe becoming emotional too. Remember, good negotiating is counter instinctive.

If it's not a tactic, and you may never know, remember to separate the people from the issues, and the people or person from their behaviour. They have their own reasons for this response. Don't buy into it. And yes, sometimes it's easier said than done, but do it anyway.

There was a famous case at the United Nations many years ago when a Russian leader became very emotional, so much so that he started to beat on the table in front of him with a shoe. Some observers later suggested that this was no spontaneous outburst, but rather it was a calculated and planned tactic, even down to there being a third shoe in the Russian's briefcase that day. He didn't even have to bend down to take his shoe off.

Another counter to this tactic is to remind them of the original agree-to-agree frame set at the beginning. Remind them that such behaviour is not congruent with this agreement, and that it's not acceptable to you. Remember though to refer to the behaviour and not to the person, and to reiterate that your combined objective is to create a win/win outcome.

Negotiating Ploy # 16
PRECEDENTS

Let's talk now about the Precedent Tactic. This is where the person with whom you are negotiating says something like: "But why should I have to do this, I know for a fact that Frank Smith didn't have to. So why should I have to?" In other words, they are claiming that there is a precedent here — a previous case. Sometimes, that will stop even the most skilled negotiator in his or her tracks. So what can you do? What is the counter gambit?

The counter gambit is to insist on the uniqueness of the case in hand: "Then was then, now is now. The circumstances are entirely different." (By the way, be prepared to rationalise and back up this assertion.)

Negotiating Ploy # 17
THE WITHDRAWN OFFER

This is a very powerful tactic which is a little like the Walk Away Tactic. It can be used at any time during the negotiation and I've even seen it work very effectively where negotiations have stalled, and one party has stopped talking, or has used the walk away tactic.

This Withdrawn Offer Tactic involves suggesting the removal of concessions or agreements already made — threatening to take away what you've already offered: "I'm sorry, the sales manager has just informed me that we've misquoted, the price I've given you is too low. I'm going to have to withdraw that offer."

You may well get an immediate response: "I'm sorry, it's too late. You can't do that. We're accepting your offer!" When you finally let them have it, they really feel that they have won. This tactic works particularly well with what we call in NLP circles, "Polarity Responders". These are people who want what they cannot have, want to do something which they are told they cannot do, must have something they are told they would not like anyway.

The counter gambit is simply to walk away and to test the validity for this move on their part.

Negotiating Ploy # 18
THE FAIT ACCOMPLI

This is a French term for something which is finished, all over, done! Particularly when this is combined with the power of putting it in writing, it can be very effective.

A few years ago, a client of mine had to break a lease on a commercial property. He was very worried about doing this, because he had signed the lease, and the landlord was within his rights to do all sorts of things to gain compensation.

My suggested opening position for my friend, was to present the landlord with a fait accompli. He vacated the premises over the weekend and paid to have them thoroughly cleaned so that when he handed the keys back, they looked better than when he had moved in.

Over the previous weeks, he had advertised for, and found, three possible replacement tenants. On the Monday morning, he presented his landlord with a carefully written letter, explaining the dire financial situation which had caused this decision. He included a full accounting for back rent, as he was a month behind with the rent. He had debited this against his initial bond, and he also enclosed the three names and files on the potential new tenants he had found, each of whom was ready to move right in. He had even obtained deposit cheques from two of them. What could this landlord possibly say? It was all over. He had moved out. His back rent was paid and he had found three possible new tenants.

I had another client in a similar position who did advise the landlord of his problem and arrived one Monday morning to find all of his locks changed. He was locked out of his own business! Now, I'm not saying what is legally right here. I'm simply using this as an example of how a fait accompli can be used.

Negotiating Ploy # 19
THE DECOY

This tactic involves asking for something you don't really want, and which you know the other party can't possibly give, so that you can then ask for a trade off, when they say they can't do it.

A negotiator asks a plastics fabrication company, for a special packaging box: "I need this within 30 days", he says, knowing full well that this is impossible. They would need at least 90 days to supply the order. When he hears the bad news he flinches: "What? That's going to give me a distribution and storage problem. That will be very costly. I can't live with that!"

Now, like a good negotiator, he stands his ground — "Hollywoods" it — before finally saying: "Tell you what. If I can convince them to live with this 90 day delivery, you're going to have to help me with this storage cost problem. I'm going to need a 5 per cent discount to cover it. Fair enough?"

And before they know it, the other party agrees, just to avoid losing the deal. But the objective all along was to get the 5 per cent discount. The 30 day delivery was not the real issue. It was just a decoy, and a very effective one at that. Be careful of decoys in your negotiating. They are used more often than you might imagine.

Negotiating Ploy # 20
THE PUPPY DOG

This is a common term used in sales and gets its name from a real-life situation which I'm sure has been going on for decades.

One Saturday afternoon, I took my two eldest children to a movie in a large shopping complex. You know the type where there are say six or ten cinemas as part of the shopping centre.

As we approached the theatre, we had to pass by a pet shop with all those cute little animals in the front window. My daughter, Skye, was immediately drawn to the window where three puppies were playing. One in particular, noticed her and started to seek her attention. "Ah, please Dad, can't I just stroke him? Can't I just go in for a moment?" Aren't kids great negotiators? Before we knew it, we were inside and she'd fallen in love with this puppy

— helped along by her younger brother, James. "Ah, please Dad, can't I have him? He's so cute!"

Right about then the pet store manager comes over and I recognise that I'm in real trouble. He makes this wonderful caring suggestion: "Hey, it's Saturday afternoon, we're closing soon. These puppies are going to be so lonely here over the weekend. Tell you what, why don't you take him home for the weekend? If you don't like him, you can bring him back on Monday."

Now I try resorting to a higher authority. "Skye, it's your mother's decision. She'll divorce me if I let you take that puppy home!" Skye reminds me that her mother and I are already divorced.

Can you see what would happen. We take this puppy home. He gets a name. He becomes part of the family, and you simply don't take a member of the family back to the pet shop on Monday, do you now? He's yours. You've bought him.

Now, I didn't name it the Puppy Dog Tactic. I don't know who did. It probably goes back centuries or eons when it was originally called the Dinosaur Close. Nevertheless, do you get the idea?

The Puppy Dog Tactic is anything you do to get the other party emotionally involved before the negotiation is finalised. I've seen real estate sales people take a Polaroid photograph of an excited couple in front of, "their new house", when they haven't bought it yet. They take the photo home, show all their friends and become emotionally involved. This makes their commitment level higher and probably makes them more flexible around the price and settlement terms.

Photocopiers used to be sold a lot like this too. They put it in your office for an "obligation free" trial, and you'd end up owning it. It's a great tactic. It works.

The counter tactic is to not accept the offer, or if you do, understand what's going on and don't become emotionally involved, or feel in any way obligated. This is often easier said than done.

Negotiating Ploy # 21
THE CALL GIRL

Finally, I'd like to talk about a principle called the Call Girl Principle. This principle gets its name from a fairly well known fact that value of services rendered always diminishes very quickly after they are rendered. Now, I don't know this from personal experience, but it makes a lot of sense, doesn't it?

Keeping this principle in mind, reminds us that any time we make any kind of concession in the negotiation, we should ask for a reciprocal trade off right away. The favour that you did somebody before, loses value very, very quickly afterwards — it's forgotten within hours or even minutes.

This is why consultants negotiate their fees up front, rather than afterwards. Remember my plumber? Even though the client may be desperate and be prepared to pay almost anything to solve his problem beforehand, once the solution is given, the client may feel differently about paying a large fee. Afterwards the problem doesn't seem to be the really big deal it was before.

Please understand, if you start delivering your service before negotiations are concluded, what you have delivered can no longer be used as a part of the negotiation.

Well, we sure have covered a great many ploys and tactics here, haven't we? If you keep these tactics in mind as you negotiate, you'll be considerably empowered to create win/win and to defend yourself against win/lose negotiators.

Clarity really does lead to power!

Part Five

Dealing With Different Negotiating Styles

In many cultures negotiating is a real art form, like a dance, or like creating an intricate work of art, with all of the subtle brush strokes that may involve.

However, in our western culture, some people, particularly Australians, New Zealanders, North Americans and Canadians, have a lot of trouble doing this dance, and playing this game of negotiating. Why is that?

Cross-Cultural Negotiating

There are many reasons for this, but one of the most obvious to me, is that we all come from countries which are relatively "young". As a consequence, our history and our traditions are vastly different to those older cultures which go back thousands of years. Such cultures have a long and proud tradition for bargaining and negotiating — characteristics which are not very predominant or deeply etched in our culture.

If you've had occasion to negotiate with people from these older cultures, you'll know already that their style of negotiating can be different to ours. So if we are to be successful at negotiating with them, we need to understand how their style differs from ours, and what we need to do, in order to create win/win with them.

So specifically, how is their style of negotiating different to ours?

Well, I believe the easiest way of explaining this is to contrast the two styles and to set a framework which says that people from these older cultures tend to be much more "context" oriented in their negotiating. We tend to be much more "content" oriented.

What do I mean by this?

Well for us, most of the message and the meaning of our communication, and our negotiating, tends to be in the linguistics, the words that we use, while with other cultures, much of the meaning comes from the context and the process itself. By this I mean the physical environment and the process internalised within the person, or people with whom we are negotiating.

For example, let's take the people of Japan, the Peoples Republic of China, Singapore, Taiwan, and Korea. These are countries with old cultures steeped in tradition.

Japan is a densely populated country, particularly compared to ours, with a homogeneous population. Because of this, and by necessity, the Japanese tend to be focused on achieving harmony. They tend to be indirect and very formal in their communication. In this culture, status and respect for status is important. It's a hierarchical society, with very orderly, social relationships between subordinates and bosses. Also, there is little concern for personal security as the crime rate is very low. The Japanese tend to negotiate in teams, and they value the collective. When negotiating with them, we often need to explain things to these teams, over and over.

The Japanese have no word for "no". They like to avoid conflict, and as I said before, they are interested in achieving harmony. Not only do they have no word for "no", it would seem that they have no word for "yes" either.

If you look in an English/Japanese dictionary you'll find a word "hi" which loosely translated really means, "Uh-huh, I hear what you say. I acknowledge your communication", but it does not mean, "Yes, I agree with you" or "Yes, I you're right."

Rather than say, "No!" outright — which in their culture could offend and could destroy harmony — they'll say, "I'm not sure." "We'll have to think about that," or "That would be difficult!"

We need to be very careful that we don't misinterpret such phrases as meaning "maybe" or even "yes"! That's not what they mean at all.

I was with a team of inexperienced negotiators, when they came away from negotiations with a Japanese team. We all heard the same conversation and I could see that they had hope in their hearts, when in reality they had just been told, "No way Jose!"

So the Japanese are High Context negotiators. Let's contrast this with our style of negotiating, which is "High Content".

What are the factors that link Australians, New Zealanders, North Americans and Canadians? Well, we all come from countries which are not densely populated. Our countries all have an immigrant heritage too. They were populated originally by people from other countries. Thus we have a very heterogeneous population with a blending of many cultures. We also share the same Anglo Saxon legal system. We have a pioneering history, where the country was shaped by rugged individuals who went out into the wilderness to tame the country. We believe in equality, where the rights of the individual are respected. We are more often than not, on a first-name basis with the members of our community regardless of their station in life. Tradition and status are not as important to us, as they are with some cultures. Indeed in Australia, the land of the Tall Poppy syndrome, there is a tendency to rebel against status and titles.

We also have a high regard for personal and family security, rather than a concern for the collective. We are a culture more of individuals, tending to be direct and up front. Our theme songs would include, "I Did It My Way", and "I Got To Be Me". Things are either black or white, right or wrong, yes or no, with no shades of grey, and we're always in a hurry.

Contrast this with the Japanese who are more indirect, and infinitely more patient. When we talk about having a long term company plan, we talk in terms of a one-year or a five-year plan — at the very most a ten-year plan. The Japanese, on the other hand, have ten-year plans or even a hundred-year plan. So, what's a few decades of negotiating to them, in a grand plan like this? Nothing! They are coming from a different place to us when they negotiate. Their model of the world is different to ours.

So, since we are literally worlds apart, we need to understand these differences when we begin to negotiate across these two cultures. By the way, I'm going to suggest that most negotiations are cross-cultural anyway, because we all have different models of the world. Isn't it true that older people often see things differently to younger people, men often see things differently to women, and children see things differently to parents?

Specific Ideas on Cross-Cultural Negotiating

1. Remember that it's all just a game. Play the game. Don't take yourself too seriously — have fun.
2. Begin negotiations with the things you have in common. Start with the small issues and leave the bigger issues until the end. For example, if you are discussing the dollars, don't go right to the bottom line. Begin by suggesting when the payment or payments will be made. How they will be made and where.
3. Be patient and adapt to the people you're negotiating with. Flexibility is the key here. We tend to be impatient, and look at the short term, whereas the Japanese and Chinese are much more patient.
4. Ask questions (even if you know the answers) and then listen carefully. Let them talk, answer their questions too.
5. Probe options together, openly, to come up with a third, a fourth or a fifth option.
6. Allow for face saving. By the way, "face" is not the same as "self image". Self image is how we see ourselves. "Face" and "saving face", has more to do with

how others see this person, and this can be very important to those you are negotiating with. In our culture where we tend to be direct and "tell it like it is", hearing the truth and telling the truth is much more acceptable than in some cultures, where to do so, might offend. Be very careful not to cause the other person to lose face, or lose honour. Honour is everything in some cultures, where people will die defending their honour, or kill for the sake of honour.

Different Characters Within Cultures

I mentioned before that I believe that all negotiating is cross-cultural to a degree. Up until now, we've been talking about the differences in communication styles with people of different nations, but isn't it true that even when we negotiate with people within our own culture, we encounter many different types and styles of character.

For example, have you noticed how some people we meet enjoy a fast pace of life? They speak quickly, they move quickly, they think quickly and they make decisions quickly. Do you know someone in your life like that? Think about that person for a moment.

OK, that's enough!

Isn't it just as true, though, that there are other people in your world who like to move more slowly? They take their time, they don't hurry through life, they speak a little slower, they move a little more slowly, they like more time to think and make decisions. Do you know someone in your life like that? Think about that person for a moment.

So, what are we talking about here? What makes these two people different? Aren't we really talking about their *style* of communicating and the way in which they process the world?

Would these two people negotiate differently?

I often ask this question of sales people. What would happen if you were a sales person and tried to move fast with a person who prefers to move slowly? Wouldn't that person feel pressured? Indeed, wouldn't that person feel this style of sales person, was a high pressure sales type? What would happen to rapport? What would happen to the level of trust? That's right, it would go down.

Alternatively, what would happen if a sales person moved slowly with a person who likes to move fast? How would that client feel? The answer is bored, and very quickly too, and then probably frustrated! And then perhaps even angry! Again, what would happen to rapport? What would happen to the level of trust? No prizes for guessing here.

So we all process the world differently, and we all negotiate a little differently too, depending upon our own personal style. Is there any rhyme or reason to this?

The good news is, yes there is, and what is even better news is that behavioural psychologists have discovered that there are some pretty simple ways of identifying a person's style of communicating, and thus their way of thinking, which if understood can assist us tremendously in our negotiations.

Frankly this is not new. For thousands of years, man has being trying to figure out what makes one person think and behave in a particular manner, while another person thinks and behaves in a totally different way. Hippocrates talked about four temperaments:

➤ The Melancholy
➤ The Phlegmatic
➤ The Sanguine
➤ The Choleric.

In 1923, Dr Carl Jung published a book called, *Psychological Types* where he identified again, four distinct styles or types. He called them:

➤ The Intuitor
➤ The Thinker
➤ The Feeler
➤ The Sensor.

More recently, we heard from Dr David Merril, Wilson Learning, Perfomax, Integra, Integro and my friends from Southern California, Dr Tony Alessandra and Jim Cathcart. I used to bring Jim and Tony to Australia in the 1980s to present their seminars where they spoke about — you guessed it — four styles of people.

Jim and Tony called them:

➤ The Socialiser
➤ The Director
➤ The Thinker
➤ The Relater.

These are terms that I really prefer, as they are more common words, but all of these names refer to the same four basic styles.

So are there really only four styles of people on the planet? Of course not! There are an infinite number, but what these people are saying, is that all of these styles can be classified into four basic styles, with common characteristics.

Do you need to be a psychologist to understand this? Well, I used to think so because when I first came across this concept more than 20 years ago, the way it was explained to me was so complex, that I didn't fully understand it, and as a consequence, I couldn't remember it, or use it.

My company now runs programmes on this, from anything up to a day in duration. However, in just a few minutes in this book, I can give you a few simple rules that you can use to determine the style of each person you negotiate with, and some pointers on how to best negotiate with them to create win/win.

So let's keep it simple.

Have a look at the illustration on the next page. At the right-hand end of the horizontal line you'll see the word FAST and at the other end, the word SLOW.

Dealing With Different Negotiating Styles

Now look at the vertical line. At the very top you'll see the word OPEN and at the bottom, the word, SELF-CONTAINED.

Let's consider the horizontal line first. Remember those two people I had you think of before? That fast-paced person and that slow-paced person? On the horizontal line, we measure the pace at which the person we are considering moves. By that I mean the pace at which they think, speak, walk, move, and so on. Some people we meet will be at the extreme right, what we call FAST, while some will be at the other end, SLOW and others will fall at various points along the line from FAST to SLOW. Get the idea?

So this is one measure that we use to determine a person's predominant style. Now I stress *predominant* style, because it's true that some of us vary our pace, and our style a great deal, depending upon the situation.

Let's look at the other scale, the vertical scale. When considering a person's style, as well as asking ourselves: "Does this person move fast or slow?", we ask the questions, how does this person communicate? Is she open? That is, does she speak freely and openly about what's on her mind, or is she more self-contained? That is, does she keep herself to herself, not speak a lot, and it's hard to know what's on her mind?

So simply make a decision, which end of the scale is she closest to? In this way, we can classify easily observable human behaviour, into the four distinct styles.

By the way, for a little extra help, on that horizontal line at the FAST end, you'll also see the word, DIRECT. People who move fast also tend to be very direct in their communication. At the other end, the SLOW end, you'll see the word, INDIRECT. People who communicate slowly, tend also to be less direct in their communication.

Think about the two people I asked you to think about earlier, and just check this out. Am I right?

Some of those slow people, really beat around the bush before they get to the point. If you're like that person you might be saying to yourself: "Hey Wayne, don't pick on them. They're sensitive people, or they like to think before they speak, and if more people did that we'd have world peace." Well, you may be right and that brings up the question, which is better — fast or slow? Direct or indirect? The answer is, neither! One is neither better nor worse than the other, they are just different.

Let's return now to that vertical line, and I have two more words that I want you to notice. At the top, next to OPEN, is the word RELATIONSHIP. At the bottom you'll notice the word TASK. It so happens that self-contained people seem to be also very TASK-ORIENTED, while people who are more OPEN, also tend to be more RELATIONSHIP-ORIENTED, or PEOPLE-ORIENTED. So when you meet someone here are two questions you can ask yourself that will help determine which of the four styles they might be:

➤ Is this person FAST PACED and DIRECT or more SLOW PACED and INDIRECT? Then all you need to do is make a decision which end of the scale they fall on. If you find yourself saying: "Well they're kind of medium", just make a decision for now, one way, or the other.

➤ Is this person more OPEN and RELATIONSHIP-ORIENTED or more SELF-CONTAINED, and TASK-ORIENTED? Again, make a decision one way or the other.

So with just two simple questions, you can be well on the way to knowing this person's predominant style.

Socialisers

Let's put some names to these styles now, and I'd like to use the names that Jim and Tony use. In the upper right-hand corner we have the people who are FAST PACED and DIRECT, and OPEN and RELATIONSHIP-ORIENTED. We call these people the SOCIALISERS — a name that really suits this style, because this is one of the things they are naturally very good at.

Some examples of the Socialiser style that you might recognise would be people like comedian and motion picture actor Robin Williams, and some game show hosts.

Directors

In the lower right-hand corner, we have people who are still FAST PACED and DIRECT but they are SELF-CONTAINED and TASK ORIENTED. We call these people the DIRECTORS, and this is a very good description of what they like to do. They enjoy being in charge, like a director of a movie, or a company. They like to direct other people, and be in control of the action.

Some examples of the Director style that you might recognise would be people like media magnates Kerry Packer and Rupert Murdoch, Americans like Ronald Reagan, Oprah Winfrey, and "Stormin' Norman" who led the Desert Storm campaign. In the *Star Trek* series, this would be Captain Kirk, Commander of the Star Ship *Enterprise*. These are tough, bottom line people.

Thinkers

In the lower left-hand corner, we have the people who like a SLOW pace and are generally very INDIRECT in their communication, while at the same time they are SELF-CONTAINED and TASK ORIENTED like the Directors. We call this style the THINKERS. Again, this is a great way of describing their style. They are very thorough, and think things through carefully before taking action.

An example of the Thinker style that you might recognise would be that *Star Trek* character Dr Spock.

Relaters

In the upper left-hand corner, we have the people who are SLOW and INDIRECT, like the thinkers, but they are

OPEN and RELATIONSHIP ORIENTED like the Socialisers. We call them the RELATERS. Again, this is a very descriptive name, as they tend to be very good at relating to other people. They are slower and caring in their style and manner of communicating with other people.

Some examples of the Relater style that you might recognise would be Americans like Dr Marcus Welby MD — remember that old TV series? And in the newer *Star Trek* series, it would be the Counsellor character, who senses people's feelings.

So which of these styles is the best?

Again, there is no good and no bad. There just is!

Environments and Surroundings

Now, there are some other great clues that we can use to confirm that we are reading a person's style correctly. To help us, each style has certain preferences in common. For example, what would a Socialiser's office look like? As I describe this, think of people you know.

A **Socialiser's** office will tend to be a bit messy, but they will tell you that they know where everything is. They'll call it "organised chaos". It will generally be bright, decorated in loud colours, posters or startling pictures. You may also see pictures of this person in their office, along with awards, photographs of their boat, or their horse, or their car, or maybe the car they'd like to have. Socialisers tend to be a little flashy, confident, flamboyant and creative, and their home and office environments tend to reflect this. They may have all the gadgets too — laptop computer, pager, mobile phone with built-in fax, electric pencil sharpener, electronic diary and so on. They may not know how to use them, but looking good is what is important to socialisers.

What would a **Director's** office look like? It would be very formal by comparison. Generally, it would be expensively decorated, but in a no-nonsense, understated manner. Dark colours and quality would dominate. They may have an enormous desk and what I like to call a Captain Kirk Chair. You know the kind I mean, with the tall back and arm rests? The sort you could run the world from, which is how Directors like to see themselves. They will often have expensive dark-wood bookshelves, and even wall-panelling. Their desk will be clear. Why wouldn't it be? They like to delegate. Control and power are very important to them. They are achievers and get the job done fast. Their motto is, "'Tis easier to beg forgiveness, than it is to seek permission!"

What would a **Thinker's** office look like?

The Thinker's office is usually very practical. It's not flashy or trendy. A laminex desk with a steel frame is common, together with furniture that doesn't match. Looking good is not that important to a Thinker. You may see a computer on their desk, plus a calculator, a note book, spare pens and pencils. Around their walls you may see charts, graphs, a white board or a black board. In their bookcase, you may see reference books and manuals.

The **Relater's** office will often be very warmly decorated, in earthy colours. Sometimes they'll have a couch for visitors, with a coffee table to sit around, because they'll come out from behind their desk to make visitors feel more comfortable. They may have plants, a coffee percolator, even their own coffee mugs and biscuits for visitors. I've see Relaters' offices that looked more like home than many people's homes!

Clothes

There will be many physical signs that will help you to verify the style of the person you are with. How about the clothes they wear? Will different styles tend to wear different clothing? In most cases absolutely! Let's have a closer look at this.

The **Socialiser** will tend to dress flamboyantly and in a trendy manner. Men will often wear coloured shirts, and bright ties, and women bright coloured clothing. Their hairstyle and grooming will again, generally, be up with the latest fashion. Looking good and personal image, is so important to a Socialiser. They tend to shop at trendy boutiques, and buy designer labels.

Directors tend to dress more conservatively, in darker colours, navy blue and black, whether they are male or female; a white shirt or blouse immaculately ironed and the men often favour a deep red tie, or a similarly strong colour. Again they dress for power. Hairstyle and grooming is conservative; the slicked-back style like Michael Douglas in the movie *Wall Street,* or short-cropped hair will be common. Often their clothing will be expensive, and tailor designed for them.

Thinkers, being practical people, will dress in a practical manner. Often men will wear grey slacks and a white shirt; short sleeves — nylon too. Their tie will probably be that favourite one they bought 15 to 20 years ago, and hasn't it lasted well? Sure was a good decision to buy polyester! Shoes may even be grey. Fashion consciousness, will not be high on their agenda. They have more important things to think about. Sometimes, we'll find that they have all the practical accessories too, like a pager hanging off their belt, and a tape measure, a set of keys and one of those plastic pocket protectors in their shirt pocket, with six different coloured pens and pencils — never can tell when one pen might run out and that way a shirt could last seven to ten years. And where do they shop? That's right they are dressed by K-Mart, while that red light was flashing! Think about it, we all know people like this!

Relaters tend to wear earthy colours, like brown or beige, in comfortable styles. Cardigans and knitted vests are popular here too — a knitted or woven tie, a scarf and brown suede shoes. There is a lot of beige in the life of a

Relater. You see, they don't want any colours that are going to offend anyone.

And what about the cars they drive?

➤ The Socialiser — flashy, flamboyant, sporty, fast cars. Red is a popular colour.

➤ The Director — cars that project power and wealth and are often dark in colour. BMWs, Mercedes, Jaguars are a popular choice, or even Range Rovers.

➤ The Thinker — they have worked out which cars are the most practical. They generally drive very plain models, and the most popular colour is white. I like to call them "white-goods on wheels". Often they buy second-hand European cars which have a reputation for reliability and a long life. After all, they've studied the stats and done the research and comparative analysis. They take a long time to decide which car to buy, then they wait patiently for just the right one to come on the market, and then they drive it for ten years. We sometimes see them in old Renaults, Saabs or Citroens.

➤ The Relater — tends to favour very conservative cars — station wagons, vans or mini buses. Why? They often have big families and are community-minded, so they belong to clubs and associations like Boy Scouts, and they need a vehicle like this for the community work they do on the weekends. These people are the salt of the earth, they really care about others. Oh, another vehicle they like is the Volvo, and guess what colour? That's right, beige! And sometimes they are to be seen, driving in the overtaking lane on freeways and they're wearing a hat too. Beware of beige Volvo drivers who wear hats. I'm not sure why I feel that way, I just do!

Professions

And would these different styles of people, tend to be found in certain professions? Yes indeed! Mind you, there are no absolutes. These are simply guidelines.

We tend to find a lot of **Socialisers** in sales, the hospitality industry, entertainment, advertising, promotion and public relations. They love people and love working with people. Fun is very important to socialisers.

Directors we tend to find running their own businesses, or in senior management positions, within corporations. They are hard driving, high achievers.

Thinkers tend to be found in professions like accounting, law, dentistry. They may be scientists, computer programmers, technicians, and so on, where attention to detail, and thoroughness is vital.

Relaters often work in the caring professions. They may be social workers, doctors, nurses, and clergy.

Strengths and Weaknesses

And does each style have certain strengths and weaknesses? Yes it does.

➤ **Socialisers** — tend to be very good with people. They are generally enthusiastic, highly motivated and very persuasive. They are able to motivate people into taking action. However, on the flip side they may not to be very good at taking care of the loose ends. Because they are easily excited by new projects, staying focused can sometimes be a problem too. They'll have quite a few projects on the go all at the one time, and may easily lose interest if something looks better somewhere else. Time management and paperwork, are not generally their strengths.

➤ **Directors** — strengths are that they get the job done, at almost any cost to themselves and to others. They are bottom-line high achievers. However, the downside of this is that they are sometimes workaholics. They have little time for personal life, and as a consequence relationships sometimes suffer. Also, because they are so fast-paced, and task-oriented, they sometimes forget about people's feelings, and in extreme cases, leave a path of destruction behind them, with damaged and broken relationships, and hurt feelings.

➤ **Thinkers** — strengths include their extremely good attention to detail and thoroughness in almost every way. The downside of this, however, is that to be thorough they tend to move slowly. At the extreme, they sometimes suffer from "analysis paralysis", where they are so busy analysing things that they tend not to make decisions or take action. They seem to love the process, much more than the final result. Indeed, they'll tell you that this is not the final result, this is simply an interim measure, as all of the information is not yet in.

➤ **Relaters** — strengths are that they are very good with people and building and maintaining relationships. Relationships are very important to these people. They'll tell you that it's the people who count, more than the project. They are very good councillors, good listeners and are genuinely caring people. They are on all the committees and community support organisations, and there is no doubt the world is a better place as a result of these people. However, the downside is, that this causes them to move slowly and because they care so much about people, they don't like to confront people, or ask people for decisions. As a consequence, they are often used by others, and taken advantage of.

What's your style?

So by now, you've probably been thinking about your style. If not I suggest you do. What is your predominant style? Are you fast-paced or slow? Are you relationship-oriented or task-oriented? Think about your office or home environment, the car you drive or would like to drive, the clothes you wear. What is your predominant style?

By the way, we all have secondary styles too, and sometimes our styles vary, depending upon the environment in which our secondary style becomes more predominant; for example, our home environment versus our professional or office environment.

Negotiating with These Styles

So how do you think these different styles might negotiate? Do you think a Relater might have a somewhat different style to say a Director? Or a Socialiser might negotiate and communicate differently to a Thinker?

Of course the answer is, yes!

What happens if you put an extreme Thinker with an extreme Socialiser? The Socialiser wants to move fast, be playful, have some fun, finalise the deal quickly and go out and have a party. The Thinker, on the other hand, wants to be sure all of the facts are taken into consideration. They want to move slowly and methodically. What will happen if we put them together in a negotiating environment, to work something out? There may be conflict.

The Thinker is likely to see the Socialiser as a "flake" — insincere, shallow, flashy and high pressure. The Socialiser may see the Thinker as dull and boring. They'd much rather watch wallpaper peeling, than be locked up in a negotiating room with a Thinker.

Similarly, the Relater and Director would have fundamental differences in values. The Director wants to get to the bottom line quickly, get the job done and move on. The Relater wants to move slower, examining all of the human aspects of the situation. He'll say: "But what about the people here? We need to consider the people and their feelings." He may see the Director as cold and heartless, whereas the Director may see him as a soft "Greenie", whose save-the-world sentiments, are out of place in the cut-and-thrust of the "real world" of business and commerce. Again, if he is not prepared to see the other person's viewpoint, there may be tension in the relationship, and conflict.

You see, all of these styles have a different model of the world. That is, they will each see the same situation from a different perspective. By the way, it's the styles who are diagonally opposite each other on our diagram, that are likely to have the most difficulty dealing with each other.

That is, unless they have developed a key ingredient, called FLEXIBILITY.

Flexibility is the Key

So why is it that some people are able to get on with almost anybody, while others cannot? The answer is that good negotiators have well developed *behavioural flexibility.*

Being flexible starts with understanding how others may perceive you and where you are coming from — your style of communicating, and thus your style of negotiating. Understanding how the person you are negotiating with prefers to communicate, will assist you in being in rapport with them and, if you are flexible enough in your style, to move towards them and their style.

For example, if you are normally a Relater, and you are dealing with a Director, understand that they probably will not appreciate your sharing, caring approach, and may not like your pace of communicating, which to them is far too slow. They may perceive you as weak and not respect you. However, if you were able to move faster and just for them, focus initially more on the factual issues, rather the people issues and people's feelings, you will be much more likely to gain their respect and be in rapport with them. Of course, once you are in rapport with them, which as you will recall we called "pacing" them, then you have a much better chance of "leading" them to a pace that suits you better.

So let's look at some of the aspects of each style which you may care to consider as you deal with them. We'll take each in turn.

Socialisers

Fears — They fear a loss of prestige or face in negotiation. Looking good always is important to them.

Under Tension — They will attack and be sarcastic.

They Seek — Recognition, so you may like to stroke their ego.

They Need To Know — How what you are offering will enhance their image and their status. They are also influenced by "social proof". That is, what other people have done in similar situations, and how these other people have benefited.

They Gain Security Through — Flexibility. They like lots of options to chose from.

To Support Them — You need to listen to and consider their ideas. They like you to listen.

They Achieve Acceptance — Through their playfulness and a stimulating environment.

They Like You To Be — Stimulating and interesting, anything except boring. Remember they like a fast pace.

Want To Be — Admired and have their ego stroked frequently.

Irritated By — Boredom and routine. They like lots of variety in who they speak with and where you meet.

Measure Their Personal Worth — By recognition and acknowledgment. They love compliments.

They Make Decisions — Spontaneously and very quickly. But watch out, they can change their mind just as quickly, so nail them down and get agreements confirmed in writing very quickly.

Director

Fears — They fear a loss of control. They like to feel they are in charge all the time. If they feel out of control, the tension will go up.

Under Tension — They will attack, be extremely assertive and dictatorial — Hitler-like!

They Seek — Bottom line results. They want productivity.

They Need To Know — What your proposal will do for them; the bottom line. What will it cost? Keep it brief and to the point.

They Gain Security Through — Control.

To Support Them — Support their goals. Show them how you can help them achieve their goals.

They Achieve Acceptance — Through their leadership, and by being competitive. They like to win.

Like You To Be — Brief and to the point.

Want To Be — In charge. You need to let them feel that they are, even if they aren't.

Irritated By — Inefficiency and indecision.

Measure Their Personal Worth (and that of others) — By bottom line results, and past track records.

They Make Decisions — Quickly and change them slowly.

Thinker

Fears — They fear being pressured and pushed along. They also fear embarrassment which would come to them if they made a decision and it was wrong, because they hadn't considered all of the angles and all of the data available.

Under Tension — They will become withdrawn and will go into avoidance mode.

They Seek — Accuracy and they respect people who are accurate. If they ask the time, and you tell them five past ten and it's only three past ten, they'll tell you you are wrong. Near enough is not good enough for them.

They Need To Know — Lots of detail about what you are proposing. Give them all the facts and logical reasons why it will work for them. They want to know how it will work, in detail, and they like things in writing.

They Gain Security Through — Preparation. They are normally well prepared and like other people who are well prepared too. They don't appreciate people who like to wing it. They distrust them.

To Support Them — Support their thinking. Help them clarify every little detail. Take time with them. Be patient.

They Achieve Acceptance — Through their correctness, and their thoroughness. They pride themselves on having all the facts at their fingertips, or on their computer database.

Like You To Be — Precise with them in every way.

Want To Be — Correct more than anything else.

Irritated By — Inaccuracy, time pressure, surprises and unpredictability. They don't appreciate surprises. If you bring new information to the table at the last minute, they will have to completely reassess the situation before making a decision, and this process may take as long again, as it took in the first place.

Measure Their Personal Worth — Through precision, accuracy and activity. The process is even more important to them than the outcome of a project.

They Make Decisions — Slowly and very deliberately.

Relater

Fears — Their greatest fear is confrontation, and hurt feelings, both their own and others. Hence, they don't like asking for decisions and will avoid telling the truth, if it will cause conflict. In other words, they may not say what's really on their mind, if they fear it will offend you, or hurt the relationship.

Under Tension — They will acquiesce and submit.

They Seek — To be understood and like personal attention.

They Need To Know — How your proposal will affect them personally and those they care about, which could be a great many people.

They Gain Security Through — Close relationships; the closer the better.

To Support Them — Seek to understand their feelings. Ask them questions and then really listen for their feelings, as much as their words.

They Achieve Acceptance — Through the quality of their relationships. They are very loyal people and conformity is important to them.

Like You To Be — Pleasant and personable. They want to get to know you as a person, your values, your beliefs, your philosophies, and they want to believe that you genuinely care about them, as a person, and about people in general.

Want To Be — Liked and approved of.

Irritated By — Insincerity, insensitivity, impatience and time pressure.

Measure Their Personal Worth — Through the quality and depth of their relationships, and their compatibility with others.

They Make Decisions — After careful consideration, particularly around the people and their feelings.

How do These Different Personality Types like to Negotiate?

Let's have a look now, at how these different personality styles negotiate and see how they are different, to the type of negotiator we've been talking about all along, the win/win negotiator.

Socialisers can sometimes get so excited by the negotiation that they lose focus on what's really happening. They become so emotional that when it all falls down around their ears later on, they are totally surprised: "But I thought we had a deal. You said...., then I said..., and we were both excited, weren't we?" And they discover that this excitement and vision of a glorious outcome, was not shared by the other party. It was their fantasy!

Directors can sometimes become street fighters. They play to win: "Don't give me any of that win/win stuff. Life is made up of winners and losers. I'm a winner and I know that they are going to be out to win too! So watch out. It's every man (or woman) for himself! It's a dog-eat-dog world out there!"

Relaters tend to become pacifiers. Their objective in the negotiation is not so much to win, as it is to make sure that everyone is happy. **Thinkers** are often analytical and detached, rigid and inflexible in their negotiating.

What Goals do these Types Strive For?

Socialisers strive to influence and motivate. They get so much fun out of taking a stand on an issue and then persuading people to their way of thinking. The fact that they can do this is their real victory and in many cases it is more important than the issue itself.

Directors strive to win at all costs.

Thinkers want order in the negotiation. They want to be able to sort everything out and have it all neat and tidy.

Relaters are forever seeking agreement. Their ideal outcome is to have kept everyone happy.

However, the goal of the **win/win negotiator** should be to create an outcome which is good for all parties involved.

They learn how to separate the people from the problem, and bring the people involved, with their different styles, one step back from the emotional issues, and the relationships, so they can focus on the just issues.

Win/win negotiators learn how to be soft on the people, but hard on the problem. They are flexible in their style of communicating, and have built rapport with all of the others involved, regardless of their style.

Weaknesses

Now each style has weaknesses in how they negotiate. The **Socialiser** tends to be too focused on himself and is sometimes not sensitive enough to the needs of the other people involved. He tends to rely on his ability to get people excited about what he is suggesting, believing that if he gets them excited enough, they'll go for it.

Directors sometimes take a position, and dig their heels in, and often later on when they discover that this is not really the best position for them to take, they won't relent, because that would mean losing face, backing down, and the desire to win, overtakes the logic that they see in the situation. They sometimes demand losses from the other people too. They think that unless the other person loses or gives concessions they cannot possibly call it a real win.

Thinkers sometimes tend to be too inflexible, too rigid, too detached and too set in their ways to be able to create win/win easily.

The major fault of **Relaters** is that they are too easily swayed to other people's points of view. They are too soft. They accept losses easily, believing that if they give enough concessions then, of course, the other people will do the same. Which doesn't always happen of course.

The Win/Win negotiator learns how to create options in the negotiation so nobody loses. He seeks to get people off the positions they have taken, mainly because of their personality styles, so that they can concentrate on common interests. Positions can be a long way apart while interests can be mutual.

The key to being able to do this, lies in the understanding of the different personality types and the way they approach negotiating differently, so you can mould them into creating win/win outcomes with you.

Part Six

Common Mistakes in Negotiating

Here are the most common mistakes that I see in negotiating. Let them be a reminder to you, of the importance of not forgetting these vital aspects of every negotiation. Indeed, you may care to use them as a checklist to ensure that you use good negotiating habits.

Poor planning

Poor planning has got to be the biggest killer of most negotiations and the major reason for not creating a win/win outcome. Poor planning is the hallmark of amateur negotiators. They do no preparation at all, and it shows. Particularly in our culture there is a tendency to simply "wing it". Don't make this mistake! Take the time, do your homework and do it right.

Rushing the negotiating process

In my opinion this is the second most common reason for creating disastrous outcomes in a negotiation. Remember that negotiating is not just about reaching the bottom line in the shortest time possible. Ours is a culture where we have become accustomed to instant coffee, five-minute meals, pizzas delivered to our door in quarter of an hour, and so with negotiating, there is sometimes a tendency to want instant results. Don't make this mistake. Take your time, and get the results you're really looking for.

Setting low goals

We don't get always get what we deserve in life, more often than not, we get what we expect — and we usually expect too little. And so it is too, in negotiating. Don't be afraid to aim high.

Forgetting that good negotiating involves counter instinctive skills

Before you respond, STOP, and think. Most instinctive responses are not the best response. The best responses are often counter instinctive.

Failure to get clear on your objectives

Clarity does lead to power. Make sure you are clear about what you really want. Know your HAP. Know your LAP. If you're not clear on your destination then any road will lead you there. Make sure it's not somebody else's road!

Failure to understand the real needs and intentions of the other party

Get that X-ray vision working. Look below what the other party says and does. Seek out their real intentions, their real needs. Remember to use in-depth questions to probe these needs and intentions of the people you deal with everyday. The behaviour you see, or the words they say are not as important as their intentions and sometimes you need to dig a little to get to that.

Talking too much

Learn to listen more than you talk. Listen for the real meaning too, not just the words themselves but the meanings behind them. Use silence. It's a powerful tool. I was negotiating with a young man for the rental of some sound equipment and a sound engineer for one of our seminars in New Zealand a couple of years ago. I asked him about his rates and he responded immediately with a figure. I didn't respond. I was thinking. Before I could say anything, he offered me a discount. Again I sat quietly. I was converting those New Zealand dollars to Australian dollars in my head and I am just naturally slow doing this. Again, before I could respond, he offered me an even better deal. Again, I said nothing. He couldn't bear the silence. He jumped in again and this time offered the services of the sound engineer free. He was negotiating himself down and I hadn't even uttered a word. Remember to listen more than you talk. Don't be afraid of silence.

Failure to establish and maintain rapport

With rapport, many things are possible. Without rapport, it can be hard — very hard! Remember that rapport is an on-going process, not just something you do and then forget.

Failure to acknowledge the other person's viewpoint

Even if you don't agree, every person is entitled to their own particular viewpoint, their own model of the world. Acknowledging their viewpoint, whether you agree with it or not, shows respect and is a part of building rapport. If a person thinks that you don't understand, they will either persist, in an attempt to make you understand — which may stall the negotiation — or they may quit out of frustration. Being understood and acknowledged is a basic emotional need of every human being.

Not allowing the other person to win

This is one of the basic criteria for creating win/win. Be careful not to back the other person into a psychological corner, with no way out. Even if they now decide to change their mind, it will be very difficult for them to do so, while keeping face. What happens when police do this with rioters? What if there is no way out? No way to save face? It's called attack! Even the nicest people will attack if there is no way out. And so it is too, in negotiating. A few years ago I was negotiating with a Chinese lady in Hong Kong, in a retail shop. I had already negotiated a very good deal, but I decided just for fun, to press a little more, just to see how much further she could really go. So I suggested that I could pay cash and thus save her the credit card commission, and also I didn't need any of the packaging materials, or any of the wrapping either, so she could now afford to give me a further discount. But she responded by saying that she was very sorry. She had now reached her very best rock bottom price. She even explained that this price included all of her overheads, like her rent, her electricity, her wages, her advertising. She explained that if she went any lower, she would lose on the transaction. Now if I continued to press harder, she was in a corner, with nowhere to go. She could not give any further concessions without losing face. But since I believe that every negotiation is just a game, I decided to keep playing it, just to see what would happen. But after some time, the lady was still "hanging in tough". And then I remembered something that another Chinese retailer had told me the morning before. I asked the lady what time it was. She said that it was 9.15 am. I said to her: "Isn't it true that your first sale of the day is a sign of good luck for rest of the day, whether it is a profitable sale or not?" She said yes, that this was the tradition. So all I had to do was remind her that I was the first sale of the day and that allowed her to win and to save face too. You must remember to always let the other person win.

Giving away too much information

During a negotiation with a group of financiers a few years ago, I suggested we take a break and we all got up from the table and went outside to another area where we could have coffee. As I chatted with one of the members of our team, I couldn't help but hear two members of the other team talking about the negotiation, not three feet away. We couldn't help hearing either, as they began to speak loudly and were obviously in disagreement on a part of the negotiation. As we listened, they began to reveal information which I had been seeking at the negotiating table, but which nobody was prepared to give. So the lesson here, is be very careful about what you say, and where you say it. Because we were no longer at the table, it was almost as if they thought we were no longer negotiating. In that break we came across information which completely changed the outcome of that negotiation.

Remember that information is a source of power. Don't give away more than you need to, unless through giving it, you are empowered in some way.

Making the first offer

Remember that unless you feel the other party's expectations are greatly mismatched with your own, it is unwise to make the first offer. Instead elicit their offer first.

Accepting the first offer

It's a big mistake to accept the other party's first offer. There is always a better offer available. Learn to flinch: "You'll have to do better than that!" Also it sets up a response of: "I could have done better than that!" in the other party.

Making the first concession

Always encourage the other party to make the first concession.

Making two or more concessions in a row

When you agree to make a concession, always get something in return. A concession from you deserves a concession from the other party. Ask for it and keep score.

Forgetting that concessions are to be traded, not given

If you give something, remember to get something back.

Being too fair and giving your best deal up front

If you do, you'll have no room to manoeuvre. If you are then pressed and can't make any concessions, the other party may not feel that they have won. Remember that people appreciate most what they have had to work for.

Being too concerned about being liked

I've seen people who make a habit of not asking for what they really want out of a negotiation, or even a relationship, because they seek the approval of others. Being liked is more important to them, than being true to themselves. In the end, they have finished up not liking themselves, and that's a heck of a price to pay.

Being too predictable

This habit cost me at least half a million dollars that I am aware of — probably more — before I realised how costly it was. Be a little unpredictable and provokable in your life and see how things change.

Underestimating your own power

You now have the tools from this book to be a way above average negotiator. Using these skills with give you more power than you have ever known. You now also understand Sources of Power (see Part Three), and can see those which empower you. You also know now that power is a perception! If you think you have it, you have it, and you always have more power than you think you have.

Underestimating or overestimating the other party's power

Both can be fatal. Don't make this mistake. Use the tools you've been given to check out the sources of power that you now understand, and never make the mistake of assuming.

Assuming that the other party understands your weaknesses

In most cases they don't! The only way that your weaknesses can empower the other party is if you let them. You do this by firstly seeing them as a weakness yourself, and then behaving in a manner consistent with this belief, or even explaining your weakness to the other party. I saw a lady do this recently in a real estate office, when she was trying to rent an apartment. She had recently separated from her husband and vacated a rented home. It had not been a quiet separation and she revealed problems with her previous landlord because of the separation. She now had no firm employment, two dependent children and was desperate. Revealing these "weaknesses", which is clearly how she saw them, made it unnecessarily difficult for her to negotiate a good rate in a suitable property.

Not understanding and recognising tactics and counter-tactics

A ploy perceived is no longer a ploy. Learn to watch out for such tactics and practise using the counter-tactics that you've been given in this book.

Forgetting that you have something they want

Always remember that negotiating is a two-way affair. The pressure is on the other person to compromise as much as it is on you. For example, the loan officer at a bank has a monthly quota to loan money. In some cases his bank spends millions of dollars every year to get people like you and I to go down to our local branch to borrow their money. He or she wants to do business with you; needs to do business with you. Reframe how you see the other party. They need you as much as you may need them, perhaps even more!

An employee goes in to see her boss and she's thinking: "I sure hope he doesn't get angry with me. Hey, I could get fired." Meanwhile, her boss is often thinking, "Hey, I hope we don't lose Sarah over this." Remembering that negotiating is always a two-way street, will empower you during the negotiation.

Failing to get an agree-to-agree frame

Don't forget this vital step. It will help prevent the negotiation coming to grief later on. If it goes off the rails, you can simply remind the other party of your original agreement, to concentrate on the issues and not the personalities; to work together to create a positive outcome for both parties, and so on.

Being pushed by time pressure

Remember that most deadlines are arbitrarily set. They can be changed and they can be exceeded. In most cases the world doesn't end if a deadline is ignored. Remember that most people become more flexible as a deadline is approached and even more so, when it passes. They feel pressured. Don't make this mistake yourself, and be careful that you don't put time pressure and deadlines on yourself.

Being intimidated by emotional outbursts

Understand that such outbursts are often just a ploy. Don't be intimidated. Stay calm, don't get caught up, don't take it personally.

Being afraid to admit mistakes and withdraw an offer already made

If you discover that you've made a mistake, don't be afraid to admit it and if necessary, change agreements already made. Again, this is counter-instinctive. Most people will not admit mistakes, and will not make corrections.

Using threats and intimidation

Sometimes as a tactic this can work wonders, but in most cases you will do much better negotiating with the other person so that in the end, they want to do what they've agreed to do. One of the biggest problems with using intimidation, is that once you're gone, the person who was feeling intimidated will not follow through with the agreement made. Future revenge also becomes a factor too, and getting even can be a powerful motivator. I always prefer to leave people feeling either that they've won, or at the very worst, "neutral" towards me. This is preferable to leaving them with a negative emotional charge. I've seen fierce competitors created by business people, who used intimidation as a tactic on a staff member they fired, or a weak competitor that they sought to destroy in a deal. Such tactics require very little skill, finesse or elegance. You can do better!

Not understanding where you are at in the negotiation

Now that you understand the structure of a negotiation (see Part Two), you'll never make this mistake again.

Stopping at an impasse

So many negotiations stop before they really gather momentum. You now possess the skills to deal with an impasse and prevent it becoming a dead lock.

Not being able to handle objections

Again, you now have the skills to smoke out the real objection, the real problem and then deal with it skilfully

Not confirming in writing quickly

This is a sure-fire way of having an agreement come undone and end in disaster with ill feeling. Invest a few minutes and take the time to put all agreements in writing.

Forgetting to practise these techniques in real life situations everyday

Make negotiating a way of life, something that you do every day, rather than something that you do on special occasions. It's often the little negotiations that improve the quality of our everyday life. Why not for example negotiate upgrades to business class or first class on the airlines? Why not ask for upgrades at hotels? A suite for the same rate as a regular room is so much nicer. A bigger car from the rent-a-car company for the same as a compact.

I was picking my car up at a parking station recently and just for fun I flinched when the attendant asked for $12. "OK, make it $8!" was his response. Negotiating is fun, isn't it?

These are the most common mistakes that I see in negotiations and they need not be a part of your negotiations any more.

Part Seven

Putting It All Together

We've covered so much ground in this book and there is always so much to continue learning about negotiating.

If you were a little new to negotiating when you started reading, then I hope you've gained many new skills.

If you were already a skilled negotiator, then I hope that it has been a journey of rediscovery for you, with many finer distinctions on what you knew already, and I trust that you picked up many new ideas too.

However, it's what you *do* now with these ideas and skills that matters. Let's summarise some of the key points so that you are able to put it all together.

Preparation phase for negotiating

1. Know what your own bottom line is (your LAP) before you begin.
2. Get clear on your "best scenario" outcome (HAP).
3. Get clear on what you really want: Must Haves, Like to Haves, Nice to Haves.
4. Consider what the other person might want.
5. Consider how far apart you might be.
6. Consider what the real motivation or intention might be behind their requests.
7. Think about how you can make them feel they've won.
8. Consider the worst possible outcome. Can you survive it?
9. Decide what issues you want to cover.
10. Consider timetables — theirs and yours.
11. Work out your opening position.
12. Work out what concession you could make if you needed to.

13. Conduct some background research on the other person.
14. Consider what sources of power you both might have.
15. Question all assumptions you may have made.
16. Consider the best location for the negotiation.
17. Be sure you are involving all decision makers and influencers.
18. Consider their negotiating style so you won't be surprised.
19. Consider how they might react.
20. Decide what style will empower you most as you play the game.
21. Consider the short- and long-term impact of your strategies.
22. Think about any legal implications.
23. Find out if there are any precedents.
24. Consider if you are the best person to do this negotiating.

Rapport phase

Anything you do which *minimises the differences* and/or *maximises the sameness.*

Matching and mirroring and leading

Body language — facial expressions — gestures — voice tonality, tempo, pace, volume, intensity — phraseology — representational systems (auditory, visual, kinesthetic) — breathing.

Gathering information

Some questions you might ask:

1. So where are you coming from?
2. How do you see the situation?
3. How do you see that this has come about?

4. Ideally, what would you like to see come out of our discussions?
5. Why do you want that?
6. How do you mean?
7. Why is that important to you?
8. What would that mean to you?

Probing options phase

➢ "Before we really get down to business here, could we first talk about some of the options available to both of us?"
➢ "May I just ask, what would you ideally like to see as the outcome of our discussions here today?"

Remember to "flinch": "What? You want what?" or "You're joking, right?"

➢ "So why would that be important to you?"
➢ "Why is that?"
➢ "How do you mean?"

Remember that dumb is smart in negotiating!

➢ "What if that were not possible? What would the next best outcome be as you see it? What would we then have to do?"

Put forward your requests:

➢ "Well, I'm just talking theoretically here now, but just suppose for a moment that I was looking for..."

And state your ideal scenario here.

➢ "How would *you* feel about this?"

Smoking out the real objection or problem

➤ **Step 1** — "Obviously you must have a reason for saying that. Do you mind if I ask what it is?"
➤ **Step 2** — "Supposing for a moment that wasn't a problem, then in your opinion do you feel this option would be possible?"

Trading concessions

➤ **Seeking concessions** — "I need......because I......"
➤ **Giving concessions** — "OK, I will agree to accept......because I......providing you agree to......OK?"

Nailing down the agreement

➤ Put as much as possible in writing.
➤ *You* be the one to put it in writing.
➤ Confirm every detail.
➤ Build in a default agreement.

Twenty sources of power

1. **Your attitude**

High need	Low need
=	=
Low power	High power

Power is a perception. If you think you have it, you have it!

2. **Your commitment**
The person most committed to their outcome is likely to achieve it.

3. **Your strategy**
Being clear on your strategy before beginning

negotiating is like having a "road map" before you start your negotiating journey. Without a map, there is no telling where you might end up.

4. Legitimacy power
This comes from anything which validates, e.g. anything in writing such as price lists, company "policies", price tags.

5. Information power
The more information you can gather on the other party, the more power you are likely to have in the negotiation. For example, why does the other party want what they are asking for? Do they have a deadline?

6. Time power
High time pressure	Low time pressure
=	=
Low power	High power

Avoid time pressure and don't be intimidated by deadlines. Give deadlines!

7. Risk power
High willingness to take risks	Low willingness to take risks
=	=
High power	Low power

A willingness to take risks gives you power. For example, if you are prepared to risk losing the deal altogether, then you have considerably more power then if you are not prepared to take this risk.

8. Options/alternatives power
Many alternatives	Few alternatives
=	=
High power	Low power

9. Walk away power

"I care...but not that much!" Once you are so emotionally involved that you cannot walk away, you are very vulnerable and much more likely to agree to the demands of the other party. Remember, there are always alternatives that are just as good if not better if you take the time to look for them.

10. Rapport power

It's easy to be tough on a stranger. It's hard to be tough on a friend. When you build rapport with the person you are negotiating with you are much more likely to gain concessions and get what you want.

11. Competition power

"I have others I could deal with." Get lots of quotes, brochures etc. when you are buying and make sure the person you are negotiating with gets to see that you have them.

12. Title power

Don't be intimidated by titles. They mean nothing unless you attach some mysterious power to them. Using an impressive title yourself, however, may make you feel more confident and may intimidate the other person.

13. Reward and punish power

This is the ability to reward and/or punish. People will be really nice to you if they believe you can do something nice for them.

14. Charisma power

Some people have the ability to charm others — think of John F. Kennedy. Use this power if you have it, and be careful of those who attempt to charm you.

15. Expertise power

This comes from what you know or are perceived to know. It may not even be real! A famous confidence trickster in the 1970s managed to travel all over the world for years seated in the "jump seat" behind airline pilots in 747s. He wore an airline pilot's uniform and phoney ID and claimed he was off duty, "dead heading" home. He was never challenged because of his perceived expertise. Pilots even asked his advice on cockpit techniques. Fortunately, he declined to give them any!

16. Environment power

Choose the location carefully. Negotiating in an environment where you feel comfortable will give you a definite edge.

17. Health and well-being power

Never negotiate when you are tired or unwell.

18. Situation power

Sometimes circumstances give a person power. Change the situation or circumstances of your meeting and you may remove this source of power. For example, the person behind the luggage check-in counter at the airport has considerable power only because of their situation.

19. Referent power

President Ronald Reagan had it, Clinton does not. It comes from being consistent and not wavering, even in the face of opposition.

20. Unpredictability power

Don't be predictable. If your actions and responses are predictable you are likely to be easily manipulated.

Ploys, gambits and dirty tricks

A ploy perceived is no plot at all.

➤ **Reluctant Buyer/Seller** — "I care, but not that much!"

➤ **The Nibble** — "...plus of course $50 delivery" or "of course, that does include delivery, doesn't it?"

➤ **Countering the Nibble** — "Oh, come on now, you've negotiated a fantastic price here, don't make me throw that in too! Fair enough?"

➤ **The Flinch** — "*How* much? That's a lot of money!"

➤ **The Higher Authority Gambit** — "I'm sorry, I can't authorise that."

➤ **Countering the Higher Authority Gambit** — "So who could authorise this?"

➤ **The Bottom Line Gambit** — "I really appreciate all the time you've spent with me, and all the work you've put in, but it's just not what I'm looking for. I'll probably end up with something smaller, I just don't need everything that yours has... But, to be fair to you...what's the very lowest price you would take?"

➤ **The Vice Gambit** — "I'm sorry, you'll have to do better than that!"

➤ **Countering the Vice Gambit** — "Exactly how much better than that will I have to do?"

➤ **The Good Guy/Bad Guy Gambit** — "Look, why don't you tell me what you can do and I'll see what I can sort out with him for you."

➢ **Countering the Good Guy/Bad Guy Gambit** — "Hey, come on you two, you're not going to try that 'good guy/bad guy' stuff on me, are you?"

➢ **The Set Aside Gambit** — "Let's just set that aside for a moment and see what else is important to both of us. Fair enough?"

➢ **The Hot Potato Gambit** — "But I have a budget of just $..."

➢ **Splitting the Difference** — "So you want $9,000 for this car, and my budget only stretches to $8,000. What a shame we can't get together on this when we are only $1,000 apart... It's a real shame, I wonder what we could do?"

Have them suggest that you split the difference.

"How do you mean? Do you mean, you're saying $9,000 and I'm saying $8,000, so what you're saying is that you'll agree to $8,500?"

Seller: "Yes, I suppose so. Hey, why not?"

"Sounds fair to me. Hopefully we can get together at that. I'll have to check with my wife first though. May I use your phone?"

After resorting to higher authority: "Well, I really tried, but I'm sorry, she said not a cent above $8,000. What a shame...what a shame. And we're only $500 apart."

Seller: "Well, I tell you what, why don't we split the difference on that $500? Do you think she'll go for that?"

"So what you're saying is that you'll agree to $8,250?"

Seller: "Yes, why not. Do you think you can get her to go for it?"

➤ **The Trade Off** — "If I can do this for you, what can you do for me?"

➤ **The Funny Money Gambit** — "Did you know that for an extra $3 per day you could enjoy the luxury version of this, with all those extras you liked so much. How about it? Your comfort is worth $3, isn't it?"

➤ **The Walk Away Gambit** — If you are not prepared to walk away, you have probably lost your power.

➤ **Delaying and Stalling** — can create time pressure.

➤ **The Pre-Condition Tactic** — "Look, if you're prepared to make me your sole distributor for this region, then and only then am I prepared to start talking with you."

➤ **Countering the Pre-Condition Tactic** — just begin negotiating anyway.

➤ **Personal Attacks** — If this happens don't get emotionally involved or lose your cool.

➤ **The Precedent Tactic** — "I know for a fact Frank Smith didn't have to do this. So why should I have to?"

➤ **Countering the Precedent Tactic** — "Then was then, now is now. The circumstances now are different. This is a different situation entirely!"

➤ **The Withdrawn Offer Tactic** — "I'm sorry, we've misquoted, and I've quoted you too low. I'm going to have to withdraw that offer."

➤ **The Fait Accompli** — when someone just goes ahead and assumes an agreement has been made.

➤ **The Decoy Tactic** — asking for something which is impossible, in order to gain a smaller concession as compensation.

➤ **The Puppy Dog Tactic** — when someone is encouraged to take it home, try it out and bring it back if they are unhappy. It creates emotional involvement and commitment.

➤ **The Call Girl Principle** — the value of a service always diminishes very quickly after it is rendered. Always negotiate fees up front, rather than afterwards.

Dealing with different negotiating styles

➤ **The SOCIALISER** — wants to move fast, be playful, have some fun, finalise the deal quickly and go out and have a party.

➤ **The THINKER** — wants to be sure all of the facts are taken into consideration. He or she wants to move slowly and methodically.

➤ **The RELATER** — wants to move more slowly, examining all the human aspects of the situation. He or she will say, "But what about the people here? We need to consider the people and their feelings."

➤ **The DIRECTOR** — wants to move fast, is interested in the bottom line, wants to be in control.

Flexibility is the key to negotiating with each style.

Common negotiating mistakes

1. Poor planning.
2. Rushing the negotiating process.
3. Setting low goals.
4. Forgetting to use counter instinctive behaviour.
5. Failure to get clear on objectives.
6. Failure to understand the real needs and intentions of the other party.
7. Talking too much.
8. Failure to establish and maintain rapport.
9. Failure to acknowledge the other person's viewpoint.
10. Not allowing the other person to win.
11. Giving away too much information.
12. Making the first offer.
13. Accepting the first offer.
14. Making the first concession.
15. Making two or more concessions in a row.
16. Forgetting that concessions are to be traded, *not* given.
17. Being too fair and giving your best deal up front.
18. Being too concerned about being liked.
19. Being too predictable.
20. Underestimating your own power.
21. Under- or overestimating the other party's power.
22. Assuming the other party understands your weaknesses.
23. Not recognising tactics and counter tactics.
24. Forgetting that you have something they want.
25. Failure to get an "agree to agree" frame up front.
26. Being pushed by time pressure.
27. Being intimidated by emotional outbursts.
28. Being afraid to admit mistakes and withdraw an offer.
29. Using threats and intimidation.
30. Not understanding where you are at in the negotiation.
31. Stopping at an impasse.
32. Not being able to handle objections.
33. Not confirming in writing quickly.
34. Forgetting to practise these techniques in real life situations every day.

Finally, here are the traits to develop to become a superb negotiator.

Character traits to develop

A TOP GUN Negotiator will:

➢ Remember that we all negotiate every day of our lives.
➢ Keep in mind that negotiating is not just about the bottom line. It's about the whole process. It's about creating a relationship where you get what you want, while helping the other person get what they want.
➢ Always remember that there are six distinct stages in every negotiation:

The counter instinctive model of negotiating
1. Preparation
2. Rapport
3. Gathering information
4. Probing options
5. Trading concessions
6. Nailing down the agreement

➢ Seek to create win/win outcomes where both you and the other party feel good about the outcome.
➢ Always feel good about negotiating and look for opportunities to negotiate.
➢ Remember that it's not necessary to seek approval, be liked or be totally reasonable in a negotiation. To do so can be dangerous.
➢ Be aware that provokability and unpredictability are useful tools.
➢ Understand that confidence comes from developing and using good negotiating skills and habits.
➢ See negotiating as just a game.
➢ Believe that everything is negotiable.
➢ Learn to use counter instinctive thinking and responses.

➤ Remember that we negotiate with people, not organisations.

➤ Look beyond the obvious and seek to understand the real motivation and intention behind other people's demands.

➤ Be totally focused and present while negotiating.

➤ Exercise your sensory acuity while negotiating, looking at body language as well as what is being said verbally.

➤ Always know what you want before beginning.

➤ Know your bottom line, your "walk away" point before negotiating.

If you take these ideas and put them into practice, then I'm sure that you'll create many success stories, many win/wins. When you do, I'd like to hear from you.

Please write to me, or telephone me. I'll always take the call or write back to you.

I can be contacted at:

TOP GUN® Business Academy Pty Ltd
2 Chamberlain's Lane
Sandringham
Victoria 3191
Australia
Tel: 61-3-9521-0500
Fax: 61-3-9521-0499

I've been honoured that you have spent this time with me.

Thank you.